HUMAN RESOURCE MANAGEMENT
IN THE BRITISH ARMED FORCES

Human Resource Management (HRM) has become a major issue for the UK Ministry of Defence and the British Armed Forces. Much emphasis is now placed on 'people issues' and these will grow in importance as the full effects of the 1998 Human Rights Act and the implications of the Macpherson Report begin to hit home. This is particularly the case for the Services, who until recently had been exempt from the main bulk of European legislation dealing with human resource and employment matters.

To date, there has been little academic investigation into HRM and the British Armed Forces. This book is the result of a conference organised by the Department of Defence Management and Security Analysis, Cranfield University, Royal Military College of Science.

The conference addressed the growing importance of HRM in the Armed Services, recognising that the time was ripe to address some of the challenging human resource issues impacting on the forces today. As well as concentrating on how the Services have dealt with recruitment and retention difficulties, it addressed such issues as diversity, equality, homosexuality and career development.

This book offers some insights into how these issues have been dealt with by the MOD and the Services. The studies are practitioner based, set within analytical academic frameworks. In the belief that our approach will open the debate in this area and encourage further research and analysis, we have set out to make each chapter educational, informative, and, we hope, challenging.

T0330916

HUMAN RESOURCE MANAGEMENT IN THE BRITISH ARMED FORCES

Investing in the Future

Edited by

Alex Alexandrou, Richard Bartle
and
Richard Holmes

LONDON AND NEW YORK

First published in 2001 in Great Britain by
FRANK CASS PUBLISHERS

Reprinted 2004 by Frank Cass
2 Park Square, Milton Park, Abingdon, Oxon OX14 4RN

Simultaneously published in the USA and Canada
by Frank Cass
270 Madison Avenue, New York, NY 10016

Transferred to Digital Printing 2006

Frank Cass is an imprint of the Taylor & Francis Group

British Library Cataloguing in Publication Data
A catalogue record for this book is available from the British Library

Library of Congress Cataloging in Publication Data
A catalog record for this book has been requested

ISBN 0–714–65128–1 (hbk)
ISBN 0–714–68156–3 (pbk)

Contents

The Authors

Alex Alexandrou has worked extensively in the field of industrial relations and human resource management, particularly in the public sector. He is now a Cranfield University lecturer in the Department of Defence Management and Security Analysis at the Royal Military College of Science, specialising in HRM from a public sector perspective.

Richard Bartle was an Army Officer for 23 years whose duties included being an Inspector of Army Training. He retired in the rank of Lieutenant Colonel and is now a Cranfield University lecturer in the Department of Defence Management and Security Analysis at the Royal Military College of Science. He specialises in Organisational Behaviour and Human Resource Management in the military sphere.

Gordon Bruce joined the Royal Air Force in 1987. He is currently a Squadron Leader desk officer in the Service Personnel Policy (SPPol) area of the Ministry of Defence having previously served in various RAF appointments as an 'HR practitioner'. As part of the SPPol Strategy team he has been involved with the production of the Armed Forces Overarching Personnel Strategy.

Graham Complin joined the Royal Signals in 1979 as an apprentice and was commissioned in 1986. Following the completion of studies at the Canadian Staff College and the Royal Military College of Science he is currently posted as a Major to Headquarters Land Command with responsibility to provide operational Communication and Information Systems advice to the Land Operations Group. His main area of interest is the development of military HRM.

Richard Douglas was commissioned into the Royal Army Educational Corps in 1981 after two years as a secondary school teacher. Since then he has been involved in the delivery, design and management of training in the Army in the UK, Germany and Hong Kong. He currently holds the rank of Lieutenant Colonel and in 1999 was appointed Commandant of the Tri-Service Equal Opportunities Training Centre at Shrivenham.

Richard Holmes is Professor of Military and Security Studies at Cranfield University, Royal Military College of Science. He taught military history at RMA Sandhurst for many years and has written a number of books including *Firing Line*. He regularly writes and presents television documentaries: his BBC 2 series *The Western Front* was screened in the summer of 1999. A Territorial infantry officer for over thirty years, until late 2000 he was Director of Reserve Forces and Cadets in the MoD.

Asifa Hussain is a MoD Research Fellow at the Scottish Centre for War Studies, University of Glasgow. She is an academic advisor to the Ministry of Defence on human resource management and equal opportunities in the Armed Forces. She is employed jointly by the MoD and the University of Glasgow. Her current research has centred on ethnic minority recruitment and equal opportunities in the uniformed services, and more significantly an analysis of ethno-religious perceptions of the Armed Forces among Britain's minority communities.

Allan Ross was commissioned in the Royal Air Force in 1982. He retired in the rank of Squadron Leader before taking up a post with the Royal Saudi Arabian Air Force. He is now a lecturer in law at Cranfield University in the Department of Defence Management and Security Analysis where he specialises in the impact of national and EC law on the military.

Introduction

Human Resource Management in the Armed Forces continues to grow in importance. This has been highlighted by the emphasis placed on 'people issues' by the Strategic Defence Review (1998), the launch of the Tri-Service Equal Opportunities Training Centre in 1998, the MoD's Mission Statement (1998), the 1999 Defence White Paper, the Social Code of Conduct (2000) and the Armed Forces Overarching Personnel Strategy (2000).

In addition, the implications of the Human Rights Act (1998), the Macpherson Report (1999) and the recruitment and retention difficulties currently being experienced by the forces suggests that now is the time to address some of the challenging human resource issues impacting on the Armed Forces today.

Because of the pace of change, at this point in time, the literature in this area lacks a cogent explanation of the cumulative effects that these changes and initiatives have had on the Armed Forces. The aim of the book is not only to examine how the constraining demands and the contraction of core personnel have affected and directed the human resource strategies of the Armed Services, but also how they are coping with the new realities and challenges. Topics of special interest include, recruitment and personal development and issues of diversity and equality.

We will examine how the MoD and the three services have tackled the sensitive issues of homosexuality, recruitment of ethnic minorities, training of service personnel to deal with equality issues and the future role of the reserve forces. In addition, the issues of personal and professional development of service personnel will be considered, in the light of recent proclamations by the MoD that the Forces should be a 'learning organisation'.

We hope that this book will not only be informative and bring the subject matter up to date, but highlight issues of concern. The publication has been structured to be of use to academics and practitioners alike, to fuel debate and to encourage others to research and publish in this area.

Alex Alexandrou
Richard Bartle
Richard Holmes

1

HRM in the Armed Forces: Options for Change to AFOPS

ALEX ALEXANDROU, RICHARD BARTLE AND
RICHARD HOLMES
Cranfield University, Royal Military College of Science

INTRODUCTION

The Armed Services, in common with other public sector organisations have experienced rationalisation and restructuring on a large scale during the 1990s. This has occurred as a result of the ending of the 'Cold War', a change in the nation's defence priorities, and various internal and external reviews, most notably Options for Change,[1] the Bett Inquiry,[2] the Strategic Defence Review (SDR)[3] and the Armed Forces Overarching Personnel Strategy (AFOPS).[4] These have been accompanied by the recent adoption and implementation of HRM practices and techniques by senior management.

Against the backdrop of such fundamental change within the Armed Forces, it is our intention to outline the major HRM developments that have occurred within the Services since 1990. As will be shown, the Forces have radically altered their traditional approach to 'people issues' by adopting and implementing some of the latest HRM practices. This has been driven by the need to update and improve internal management systems relating both to the organisation and to the 'workforce' in terms of achieving greater efficiency, rationalisation and flexibility.

Our understanding of the underlying ideology of HRM within the Armed Services is that it is dominated by the need to recruit and retain the best available talent, contraction of the 'core workforce' (i.e. armed personnel) and constraining demands on the public purse. The aim has been to deliver and yet at the same time to improve efficiency, effectiveness and flexibility. In practice, it seems to be characterised by a significant decrease in the number of service personnel, overstretch, low morale and difficulties in recruiting the next generation.

There have been a number of developments, which have had a significant bearing on HRM in the Armed Services. We would like to take as our base the Options for Change initiative and move through the 1990s and finish off with the introduction of AFOPS in the new millennium. But first to set the scene we will examine some aspects of the present manpower crisis that, arguably, has influenced HRM strategies so significantly.

ARMED SERVICES MANPOWER LEVELS, 1990–1999

To put some of the issues into context, particularly recruitment and retention, the following table shows the overall effect that succeeding initiatives have had on the manning levels of all three Services.

TABLE 1
STRENGTHS OF UK REGULAR FORCES – TRAINED AND UNTRAINED,
1990–1999

Year	Royal Navy	Army	RAF
1990	63,200	152,800	89,700
1991	62,100	147,600	88,400
1992	62,100	145,200	86,000
1993	59,400	134,600	80,900
1994	55,800	123,000	75,700
1995	50,900	111,700	70,800
1996	48,300	108,800	64,700
1997	45,100	108,800	56,900
1998	44,500	109,800	55,800
1999	43,700	109,700	55,200

Source: UK Defence Statistics, 1992–1999[5]

As the above figures clearly illustrate, all three Services have experienced downsizing on a huge scale. The Options for Change[6] and Defence Costs Studies[7] initiatives accounted for approximately 43,000 personnel between 1992–1997. This situation was exacerbated by the effects of the SDR,[8] which cut the Navy's numbers by a further 1,400, allowed the RAF to maintain existing numbers and demanded an increase in

Army personnel of 3,500. Inevitably this has had an impact on recent human resource strategies some of which we shall now examine.

OPTIONS FOR CHANGE, 1990

In July 1990, Tom King, the then Secretary of State for Defence, made the following statement to the House of Commons on 'Options for Change':

> 'Our proposals will bring savings and a reduction in the share of GDP taken by defence. We need force levels, which we can afford and which can be realistically be manned, given demographic pressures in the 1990s. The aim is smaller forces, better equipped, properly trained and housed, and well motivated. They will need to be flexible and mobile and able to contribute both in NATO and, if necessary, elsewhere'.[9]

He continued by stating that the Government was looking for substantial savings and that it envisaged that by the mid-1990s the United Kingdom would have a Regular Army of about 120,000 personnel, Royal Navy/Royal Marines of approximately 60,000 and a Royal Air Force of about 75,000. He said that he expected similar reductions in civilian numbers and announced that a decrease in the number of volunteer reserves would also be considered. According to Tom King the new force structures would give the nation strong and reliable forces that were affordable and could continue to make a significant contribution to NATO.[10]

Thus the scene was set. The initiative would save precious financial resources, reduce manpower and yet create a flexible organisation that could be deployed in different circumstances under the auspices of NATO and other international bodies, most notably the United Nations (UN).

INDEPENDENT REVIEW OF THE ARMED FORCES MANPOWER CAREER AND REMUNERATION STRUCTURES – THE BETT INQUIRY, 1995

Michael Bett's inquiry was commissioned in 1994 to look forward to the year 2010 and review the Armed Forces career and manpower structures and terms and conditions of service.

3

The review's full terms of reference were to:

> '...examine Service career and manpower structures, and terms and conditions of service, and recommend changes required to render them appropriate to the needs of the 21st Century'.[11]

The inquiry team was to take into account changes in military commitments and deployments, examine practices within the armed forces of other nations and of other organisations in the United Kingdom and propose future structures which were robust, flexible, efficient and cost-effective. It was asked to pay particular attention to current practice in such areas as length of service, career patterns, deployment patterns, rank structure and trade structures and the relationship between responsibility, rank, trade and pay. The inquiry team was also asked to examine the concept of performance pay, sources of dissatisfaction and the scope for a rationalised pay and allowance structure.[12]

The aim of the review was to make recommendations that would contribute to the reduction over the longer term of the overall costs of manpower, and identify clearly the resource implications of its proposals. It was also to take full account of the requirement to maintain disciplined, highly trained and well-motivated Armed Forces, and the particular requirements of Service life.[13]

The final report made 150 recommendations and observations covering a wide area. Of particular interest was the observation that there was no personnel policy to help manage the careers of military personnel and the informal, horizontal working practices of civilian employers were likely to be more attractive than the hierarchical and directive style of the Forces.[14] To that end Bett recommended the creation of a Services Personnel Board. He argued that too often in the present system, personnel management decisions were referred upwards '...without coming to rest with a proper authority'. He identified what he called a 'centralist culture' that 'coupled with the constant pressure of public expenditure constraints, has led to employment policies dictated by tradition and attempts to impose uniformity among the three services'.[15] Consequently, he recommended that the Treasury and Ministry of Defence (MoD) should delegate to each Service the responsibility for fundamental activities such as recruitment, retention and pay and conditions. The proposed Services Personnel Board would ensure all three Services operated within a single framework.[16]

In addition Bett felt that a Director of Service Personnel should be appointed to ensure that the Armed Forces are kept abreast of legal developments and modern training and personnel practices. He recommended that the post should be held for four years with the result that the 'day of the generalist, passing through a service's personnel department and spending a relatively short time there before moving on to another posting, should now be brought to a close'.[17]

Bett's remit was to look at pay and conditions of service, and not unsurprisingly he felt that the Services' 25 year old pay structure should change. As well as the introduction of performance related pay, the report recommended the creation of wide pay bands to enable people to be rewarded for individual skills, experience and performance while remaining in the same rank. In addition it forecast that senior officers could anticipate large rises. The report also noted the impact on changes in the Civil Service senior salary structures. It argued that if these were not taken into account then there would soon be a serious disparity between senior service personnel and civil servants that worked together and were in MoD posts which could be filled by either.[18]

It seems that the belief behind these recommendations was that the Armed Forces whilst priding themselves on their efficiency were in need of accepting outside ideas to make military service a more attractive work prospect.

It must be stated that a number of the recommendations were eminently sensible, notably the need for a 'purple' HRM strategy and organisation. Others, such as performance related pay, were lifted from the private sector and from a military perspective seemed to be the antithesis of public service and ethos. Interestingly the make up of the inquiry team was weighted in favour of private sector practitioners and was supplemented by management consultants who helped with the research, analysis and, in the later stages of the review, also assisted the team in the formulation of some of the options for 'development'.[19] This was a sure sign that the government thinking of the time was for private sector solutions for public sector problems.

THE ARMED FORCES OF THE FUTURE – A PERSONNEL STRATEGY, 1997

Essentially, this so-called personnel strategy[20] simply informed the Services that it was addressing the issues raised and the recommendations made by the Bett Inquiry. Significantly it made no firm undertakings. However, the then Minister of State for Defence, Michael Portillo, on introducing this strategy made this significant statement:

> 'At the heart of our Personnel Strategy for the Armed Forces is the need to attract and retain substantial numbers of high quality men and women, so that the Forces can continue to fulfil their operational commitments into the 21st Century. To achieve that, our personnel policies must recognise and reflect the unique demands of Service life. At the same time, they must take account of the terms and conditions of employment applicable to relevant civilian groups, respect modern practices in management and career planning, and offer careers which are satisfying and rewarding. The right terms and conditions of service are critical to achieving our operational aims'.[21]

STRATEGIC DEFENCE REVIEW (SDR), 1998

Following a year-long defence review, the present Government announced a series of measures that would see the overall defence budget reduced by £658 million. It argued that the SDR was a foreign policy-led review designed to put the emphasis on peacekeeping and conflict resolution with obvious human resource implications.[22]

The key changes contained within the SDR were:

- The reduction in the total defence budget from £22.24 billion to £21.55 billion.
- The total number of Territorial Army personnel to be reduced from 57,000 to 40,000.
- Armoured regiments to be cut from eight to six.

- Fewer destroyers and frigates and combat aircraft.
- The ordering of two new aircraft carriers and an additional four Ro-Ro ferries.[23]

Of particular interest was a whole section of the review addressing human resource issues, particularly recruitment and retention, morale, training and the various issues contributing to the Services current overstretch position. It stated that:

'We must...recruit highly motivated people. We must invest in their training. We must retain them and maintain their motivation. To do this we must equip them properly for the tasks we give them. We must also ensure that our demands on them and their families do not become unreasonable'.[24]

It pointed out that past defence reviews had concentrated more on strategy and equipment and less on its personnel and that this review would put them at the centre of the MoD's plans. The initiatives that the review described were intended to form part of a long-term coherent strategic approach to meet the Forces' requirement for high quality Service and civilian personnel.[25]

A number of supporting essays were attached to the SDR and there was one dealing specifically with 'people issues' with the title of 'A Policy for People'.[26] It recommended that policies be formulated in the following four distinct areas.

- **The Individual.** A wide spectrum of measures were unveiled including embracing the concept of lifelong learning, improving single living accommodation and various improvements in operational welfare.

- **The Family.** These included establishing a Service Families Task Force and enhancing the provision for Service Children's education.

- **Personnel Management.** In the main this involved concentrating on the issue of equal opportunities, by recruiting the best from ethnic minorities and setting up a Tri-Service Equal Opportunities Training Centre.

- **Longer Term Initiatives.** Here a wide raft of new HRM strategies was announced including the production of overarching personnel and recruiting strategies and the introduction of better career management (which will be addressed in Chapter 3). A new common appraisal system, a review of compensation and pension arrangements, a new pay system and significant changes to military discipline justice legislation and procedures were also introduced.[27]

It is fair to state that the SDR, in theory at least, paid significant attention to human resource issues in a way that no other review of the Services had previously managed. The rhetoric was full of the right language in terms of recruiting and retaining the best people from all sections of society and that its 'people strategy' should be long term taking into account the Forces' new role in terms of providing humanitarian and peacekeeping assistance. Various chapters in this book will examine many aspects of this strategy and the impact it has had on the Service personnel to date.

THE DEFENCE MISSION, 1998

Following on from the SDR, the MoD produced a statement of its defence mission. This gave strategic direction to the Services by formulating a mission statement[28] that defined the functions of the Ministry and the Armed Forces and how they intended to achieve them. Significantly, it stressed the importance of its personnel by declaring that:

'Success depends, above all, on our people. We must:

- Recruit and retain the best people for the job from a diverse society;
- Train, motivate and equip them properly;
- Manage with care, ensuring that the demands on individuals and their families are reasonable;
- Develop careers in defence and skills for life'.[29]

It goes on to point out that all this must be achieved by making every pound count. To that end it stressed the need to develop a joint approach not only amongst the services but also with civilian personnel.[30]

8

DEFENCE WHITE PAPER, 1999

The White Paper,[31] which was presented to Parliament in the last days of 1999, set out the progress that had been made since the SDR together with new issues that have arisen since the review was announced. It is a strategy paper that points the way forward in terms of future defence policy whilst at the same time it underlines the importance that the Government attaches to human resource issues and their impact on its policy.

Like the SDR it contains a whole section on 'people issues'[32] and lays out what has been achieved to date and reports on the work in progress. The majority of initiatives that have been put in place to date can best be described as day-to-day personnel issues. These include the introduction of an Armed Forces Overarching Recruiting Strategy, revising arrangements for membership of Courts Martial, working towards a Tri-Service Discipline Act, improving career transition support, increasing a number of allowances and various enhancements to Service children's education.

Of greater strategic importance in HRM terms is the work currently being undertaken by the MoD. This includes improving the provision of personal development through the Learning Forces Initiative (an area that will be examined in greater detail in Chapter 4); the development of a common appraisal system for officers; increasing recruitment from ethnic minorities and woman (both these issues will be addressed in depth in Chapters 6 and 7); and reviewing the Armed Forces compensation and pensions arrangements.[33]

The Paper reinforces the fact that the Armed Forces are different and that a balance must be struck between the operational requirements placed on them and the rights and freedoms to which service personnel should be entitled as members of society.[34] From an HRM perspective this statement has significant relevance not only as to how the Armed Forces human resources strategy is to be developed but also how it is to be implemented. Of particular importance were the specific issues of homosexuality, equality of opportunity, diversity and recruitment and retention, which will be examined in greater detail throughout the book.

CODE OF CONDUCT FOR ARMED FORCES PERSONNEL, 2000

As a result of the ruling by the European Court of Human Rights in September 1999[35] on the issue of sexual orientation and Armed Services personnel, the MoD has been forced to review its policy on homosexuality within the Forces. Until this judgement, the policy was that homosexuality was incompatible with Service life. In the cases of *Lustig-Prean and Beckett v The United Kingdom and Smith* and *Grady v The United Kingdom*,[36] the court ruled that their treatment was an infringement of human rights and that sexual orientation was a private matter. This forced the Government to review its policy and consequently, in January 2000 it was announced that MoD would conform to the judgement and would lift the bar on homosexuals joining the forces. It enshrined this judgement in a new code of conduct.[37] This issue of homosexuality, the European judgement, the code of conduct and the HRM implications of this whole issue will be discussed in greater detail in Chapters 8 and 9.

ARMED FORCES OVERARCHING PERSONNEL STRATEGY (AFOPS), 2000

One of the key recommendations of the SDR's 'Policy for People' was that the MoD should develop an Armed Forces Overarching Personnel Strategy and this came to fruition in February 2000.[38] The policy will be discussed in greater detail in Chapter 2, but it is important to note that the Secretary of State for Defence, Geoffrey Hoon, has stated that:

> 'This strategy document not only offers direction, but will also allow us to track how we are doing in practice by providing the basis for a comprehensive action plan against which our record can be judged'.[39]

CONCLUDING REMARKS

Clearly the last decade has seen a number of human resource and personnel initiatives that have had a major influence on the Armed Forces of today and will also impact on the way in which they will carry out their duties in the future. Most of these have been in response to the changing nature of military requirements and their knock on effects. However, as the White Paper and AFOPS have recognised, there are serious problems regarding recruitment and retention within the Services and as a result this will be one of the main issues to be discussed in several sections of this book. Career and personal development have an acknowledged impact on both recruiting and retention and so they will also be addressed as will the role and position of the Reserve Forces. Diversity and equality issues will be considered and the impact they have had on the Armed Services human resource strategies. These are the issues of the day as clearly highlighted by the SDR and the Armed Forces Overarching Personnel Strategy and rightly they provide a central backbone for the remainder of this book.

NOTES

1. Tom King, Defence (Options for Change), *Hansard*, HMSO, London: 25 July 1990, Columns 468–86.
2. Michael Bett, *Independent Review of the Armed Forces' Manpower, Career and Remuneration Structures*, HMSO, London: 1995.
3. Ministry of Defence, *The Strategic Defence Review*, Cm 3999, HMSO, London: July 1998.
4. Ministry of Defence, *Armed Forces Overarching Personnel Strategy*, MoD, London: February 2000.
5. Ministry of Defence, *UK Defence Statistics, 1992–1999*, London, TSO.
6. Tom King, op. cit.
7. Ministry of Defence, *Defence Cost Studies (Front Line First)*, MoD, London: 1994.
8. Ministry of Defence, *The Strategic Defence Review*, Op. Cit.
9. Tom King, op. cit. Column 468.
10. Ibid. Column 470.
11. Michael Bett, op. cit. p. ii.
12. Ibid.
13. Ibid.
14. Ibid. pp. 93–109.
15. Ibid. pp. 9–14.
16. Ibid. pp. 11–12.
17. Ibid. pp. 12–13.
18. Ibid. pp. 45–52.
19. Ibid. pp. ii and iv.
20. Ministry of Defence, *The Armed Forces of the Future – A Personnel Strategy*, MoD, London: 1997.
21. Ibid. p. v.
22. Ministry of Defence, *Strategic Defence Review*, Op. Cit.
23. Ibid.
24. Ibid. p. 31.
25. Ibid. p. 36.
26. Ministry of Defence, *The Strategic Defence Review – Supporting Essays*, Cm 3999, MoD, London: July 1998.
27. Ibid. *Supporting Essay 9, A Policy for People*, pp. 9-1–9-18.

28. Ministry of Defence, *The Defence Mission*, MoD, London: 27 November 1998.
29. Ibid.
30. Ibid.
31. Ministry of Defence, *Defence White Paper, 1999*, Cm 4446, TSO, London: December 1999.
32. Ibid. *Chapter 4, People in Defence*, pp. 29–40.
33. Ibid.
34. Ibid. p. 35.
35. European Court of Human Rights, *Judgements in the Cases of Lustig-Prean and Beckett v The United Kingdom and Smith and Grady v The United Kingdom*, ECHR, Strasbourg: 27 September 1999.
36. Ibid.
37. Ministry of Defence, *Code of Conduct for Armed Forces Personnel*, MoD, London: 12 January 2000.
38. Ministry of Defence, *Armed Forces Overarching Personnel Strategy*, op. cit.
39. Ibid. p. i.

2

Armed Forces Overarching Personnel Strategy

GORDON BRUCE
Service Personnel Policy Strategy, Ministry of Defence

INTRODUCTION

In April 2000, the Ministry of Defence implemented the Armed Forces Overarching Personnel Strategy (AFOPS). Commissioned 18 months earlier, by the Strategic Defence Review, it is designed to promote operational effectiveness by providing a statement of vision, strategic guidance and direction for Armed Forces personnel policies. At the strategic level it aims to define and progress tri-Service personnel issues (where tri-Service policy adds value) and provide guidance on single Service personnel issues where required. Below strategic level, the single Services are responsible for the implementation of tri-Service personnel policies and for the development and implementation of personnel policies in those areas where tri-Service strategic guidance is not required. The AFOPS does not seek to impinge on the individual identity and ethos of each single Service which it is important to maintain.

SCOPE

The AFOPS is primarily focused on regular Armed Forces personnel. However, the Strategy also acknowledges the contribution made to the provision of Defence capability by Volunteer and Regular Reservists and Cadets. Furthermore, the Strategy acknowledges the contributions made by both the families of Service personnel and the welfare organisations, and the increasing provision of support to ex-Service personnel.

WHY WE NEED AN AFOPS

There are five main reasons for the development of an AFOPS:

a. An organisation the size of the Armed Forces (which employs over 200,000 people and which spends over £6bn per annum on serving military personnel) should have a visionary statement setting out its approach to its people.

b. Likewise, the Armed Forces should also have a mechanism for the strategic direction of personnel issues, which would form an integral part of the Defence Strategic Plan, with detailed targets reflected in the Departmental Corporate Plan.

c. A more coherent personnel strategy would enhance the maintenance of operational effectiveness and the delivery of Defence outputs.

d. The increased diversity of the MOD organisation and the growing emphasis on joint operations and joint headquarters and units has provided added incentive for change.

e. The increasingly complex nature of the modern world, with an ever growing list of national and European regulations and directives, requires a coherent approach.

THE CONCEPT AND FIRST ORDER PRINCIPLES OF AN AFOPS

Concept. The AFOPS is a strategic approach to the management of the Services' most valued assets, the Service personnel who individually and collectively contribute to the achievement of the Departmental Objectives. It is designed to provide a clear sense of direction at the highest level of the MOD in what is an often turbulent environment, so that the Department's organisational and business needs can be translated into coherent and practical policies and programmes. It aims to encapsulate the vision and the overall direction the Armed Forces wish to pursue in achieving their objectives through people. It provides a coherent strategy for the Department to look ahead into the 21st Century.

First Order Principles. The AFOPS has been developed under the umbrella of the following First Order Principles:

- Set and owned at the highest level.

- Coherence with Departmental strategy (Defence Strategic Plan and Departmental Corporate Plan).

- Directed at maximising operational effectiveness.

- A 'Living Strategy' subject to regular review and evaluation.

- Single Service personnel strategies linked to AFOPS.

- Single Services to retain individual identity and ethos.

- Inclusion of all Armed Forces personnel, their families and personnel related organisations, who contribute to the Departmental Objectives and Supporting Objectives – the 'Cradle to Grave and beyond' philosophy.

- Coherence with the MOD Civilian Personnel Policy Statement and Strategy.

- Coherence with the Departmental aim to be an accredited Investor in People.

- Application of central standards where applicable.

- Full use of Service and modern external best practice where appropriate.

- Recognition that there will be financial constraints and of the need to be cost-effective.

Division of Responsibilities/Tolerable Variation. The division of responsibilities between the Centre and the single Services for the formulation of high-level policy in each of the personnel policy areas is a key element of the AFOPS. There are areas where the formulation of personnel policy is led by the Centre and others where the single Services are wholly responsible for the policy. However, there are Centre-led policy areas where the single Services may vary, within agreed limits, the manner in which Centre prescribed policies are implemented; this ability to vary is called 'tolerable variation'.

15

AFOPS STRUCTURE

The AFOPS comprises two parts:

a. **Main Document**

(1) **Chapter 1 – Introduction.** A 'scene setting', contextual section which lays out the background, the concepts and principles that were followed during the development of the AFOPS and the mechanisms for its delivery.

(2) **Chapter 2 – Armed Forces Personnel Policy Statement (AFPPS).** The 'visionary' section of the AFOPS which sets out the role of Service personnel in the achievement of the Department's objectives; the principles and standards expected of Service personnel; the value of the distinctive identity and ethos of the individual Services, and the vision for the future.

(3) **Chapter 3 – Personnel Strategy Guidelines (PSGs).** The 'directional' section of the AFOPS which outlines high level policy and, in particular, the guiding principles and goals in each of the Strategy's 28 personnel policy areas. The PSGs outlined in this Chapter revolve around five key themes: 'Cultivate, Obtain, Retain, Sustain and Remember'.

b. **Action Plan**

(1) **Action Plan.** The Action Plan is the mechanism by which the goals set out in the 28 PSGs will be delivered. It details the objectives/ performance indicators in each personnel policy area, providing direct linkage to the Departmental Corporate Plan. The Action Plan also highlights key aims, entitled 'Breakthrough Objectives' which are designed to meet the requirements of the Department's top priorities for Service personnel. Classified Restricted, the Action Plan is published as a separate document – for internal management use within the Ministry of Defence and the Armed Forces.

DEPARTMENTAL PLANNING PROCESS

The AFOPS is firmly linked into the MOD planning process. It is the means by which the Department's top priorities for

Service Personnel, identified in the Defence Strategic Plan, are fully articulated and given effect. It also informs the Defence Strategic Plan. The AFOPS Action Plan is closely linked to the Departmental Corporate Plan. Through the mechanism of the 'Breakthrough Objectives', the Action Plan identifies those key areas of Service Personnel business where visibility at the highest levels of the Department is necessary. The Action Plan also includes further objectives which reflect the Service Personnel Board (SPB) management priorities. The SPB is responsible for the regular review of the AFOPS. In addition, the Deputy Chief of Defence Staff (Personnel) (DCDS[Pers]) has a responsibility to consider Service personnel priorities and provide advice to senior management on the implications for Service personnel of the annual resource allocation round.

SINGLE SERVICE PERSONNEL STRATEGIES

Linked to the AFOPS are the three single Service personnel strategies.

a. **Royal Navy.** The Naval Personnel Strategy builds upon the framework established by AFOPS. It aims to establish the strategy for personnel matters in the Naval Service. Based upon 6 pillars – Organisation, Recruiting and Training, Career Management, Conditions of Service, Health, Welfare and Recreation and Recognition – it identifies the unique requirements of the Naval Service, its personnel and their families and embraces 2SL's corporate and management plans, 2SL's Personnel Functional Standards and the Naval Manning Plan.

b. **Army.** The Army's HR Strategy aims to provide the strategic framework within which coherent and effective HR policies can be actioned in order to deliver the human element of Fighting Power. It will be reviewed every 5 years or so. Additionally, the Army has developed a supporting HR Strategy Action Plan, issued annually to take forward the essential measures necessary to deliver the Strategy.

c. **Royal Air Force.** The RAF Strategy For People is based on the four pillars of 'Recruit', 'Train', 'Sustain' and 'Retain' and is linked, as in AFOPS, to a detailed Action Plan. This will be reviewed annually.

ARMED FORCES PERSONNEL POLICY STATEMENT

The Ministry of Defence is a large organisation which requires strategic guidance and direction for its Armed Forces personnel policies. This is provided through the AFOPS. The Strategy promotes operational effectiveness by providing a clear sense of direction, encapsulating top management's vision of the future for Service personnel and the overall direction the Department wishes to pursue in achieving its objectives by good management and care of its people. This Armed Forces Personnel Policy Statement (AFPPS), the 'visionary' section of the AFOPS, sets out the role of Service personnel in the achievement of the Department's objectives; the principles and standards for the management of Service personnel; the values and standards expected of Service personnel; the value of the distinctive identity and ethos of the individual Services; and the vision for the future.

Section 1 – The Defence Mission

The Defence Mission states that:

'The purpose of the Ministry of Defence, and the Armed Forces, is to:

- *defend the United Kingdom and Overseas Territories, our people and interests; and*
- *act as a force for good by strengthening international peace and security.*

To achieve this the Ministry of Defence generates modern, battle winning forces and other Defence capabilities to help:

- *prevent conflicts and build stability;*
- *resolve crises and respond to emergencies;*
- *protect and further UK interests;*
- *meet our commitments and responsibilities;*
- *work with Allies and partners to strengthen international security relationships.*

Success depends, above all, on our people. We must:

- *recruit and retain the best people for the job from a diverse society.*

- *train, motivate and equip them properly.*
- *manage with care, ensuring that the demands on individuals and their families are reasonable.*
- *develop careers in Defence and skills for life.'*

Section 2 – A 'Policy for People'

The 'Policy for People', outlined in the 1998 Strategic Defence Review White Paper, highlighted a commitment to place people at the centre of the Ministry of Defence's plans. It provided a framework for a coherent strategic approach to meet our long term need for high-quality personnel and to give them confidence in their future in Defence. This means giving Service personnel terms and conditions of service which are up to date and which strike the right balance between the needs and aspirations of the individual on the one hand and the Department on the other.

The AFOPS aims to promote operational effectiveness and provide a high-level focus for the development of coherent and practical personnel policies which are fully compatible with the concept of joint operations. Military operations are physically and mentally demanding, extremely unpredictable, and inherently dangerous. In the end they depend for success on team work, which comes from first class training, good leadership, comradeship and mutual trust. Such trust can only exist on the basis of shared values, the maintenance of high standards, and the personal commitment of every member of the Armed Forces to the task, the team, the Armed Forces and the Nation.

The Strategy underpins our need to generate modern, joint, battle-winning forces.

THE TEAM

Britain's Defence depends on the personnel who serve in the Armed Forces and the MOD civil servants and civilian contractors who work alongside them. We ask a lot of them, especially when preparing for, on or in the aftermath of operations. Ultimately Service personnel understand and accept that they, or their comrades, may be killed. The demands do not stop at the front line, they also apply to the many military and civilian personnel in the support chain.

And they affect their families. We also expect a lot of our people by way of their skills – defence is a highly professional, increasingly high technology, vocation.

To have modern and effective Armed Forces, we must recruit and retain our fair share of the best people the country has to offer from our diverse society. The quality of our people and their readiness for the tasks entrusted to them are the bedrock of our Armed Forces' operational capability. We will seek to ensure that personnel are properly led, motivated and equipped for the numerous tasks we ask them to perform. We will strive to be a modern and fair employer and have pledged ourselves to continuous improvement in all our practices. We will invest in training, developing Service careers and skills for life. Operations involve inherent risks to life and health; we will use all means at our disposal to minimise those risks, avoid unnecessary threats to health, and provide treatment, rehabilitation and after care services. Finally, we aim to manage our personnel with care, ensuring that the demands on both them and their families are reasonable.

The AFOPS is primarily focused on regular Service personnel, but also acknowledges the contributions made by the Volunteer and Regular Reservists and the Cadets, together with those made by both the families of Service personnel and the non-Service Welfare organisations. Due to the very different nature of the terms and conditions of service of MOD civilian personnel, who have their own Personnel Policy Statement and Strategy, this Strategy does not apply to MOD civilian personnel, but it acknowledges their contribution and is coherent with their Policy Statement and Strategy. Nor does it apply to other staff, such as contractors, who also have a role to play in delivering defence capability.

THE INDIVIDUAL

The British Armed Forces have a reputation second to none, based on the high standards of professionalism, behaviour, and self-discipline that they have consistently displayed, and upon their success in operations. These are not, however, qualities that can be taken for granted and the development and maintenance of such standards throughout the Armed

Forces presents a greater challenge today than in the past. The Armed Forces should reflect the society they serve, but there must also be an acknowledgement, by society and by Armed Forces themselves, of the need to be different and of the emphasis that must be placed on the core values and standards which in some respects diverge from those which obtain in society at large. Personnel have a duty to uphold the core values and standards of the Armed Forces, whenever and wherever they are serving, on duty and off. Success on operations, and ultimately the lives of their comrades, may depend on their doing so.

All Service personnel are expected to display high levels of:

- integrity (reflected in their honesty, sincerity, reliability and unselfishness);
- courage (both physical and moral);
- selfless commitment (putting the needs of the mission, and of their team, ahead of their own interests);
- professionalism and pride;
- loyalty (to their commanders, their comrades, those they command and their duty);
- self-discipline and respect for others.

They are also expected to maintain high standards of conduct. They must:

- abide by the civil law, wherever they are serving;
- abide by military law and the laws of armed conflict;
- avoid any activity which undermines their professional ability, or puts others at unnecessary or unreasonable risk, or any behaviour which damages trust and respect between them and other members of their team.
- respect and value every individual's unique contribution, irrespective of their race, ethnic origin, religion or gender and without reference to social background or sexual orientation.

The Armed Forces are striving to attain equal opportunity for all personnel. Our equal opportunities goal is:

"To achieve universal acceptance and application of a working environment free from harassment, intimidation and unlawful

21

discrimination, in which all have equal opportunity, consistent with our legal obligations, to realise their full potential in contributing to the maintenance and enhancement of operational effectiveness. The Armed Forces respect and value every individual's unique contribution, irrespective of their race, ethnic origin, religion or gender and without reference to social background or sexual orientation."

Section 3 – Identity and Ethos of the Individual Services

We recognise that people join and serve in the Naval Service, the Army and the Royal Air Force, not defence. The core values and standards of Armed Forces personnel are common, but the identity and group loyalty of each individual Service, and of ships, regiments and squadrons within each Service is the key ingredient to a successful personnel strategy which is, in itself, a vital element of operational effectiveness.

Each of the Services has a distinct ethos and identity, reflecting many decades of tradition and experience, which we must retain and cherish. However, the changing nature of warfare, with increasingly joint operations necessitating teamwork by all three Services (and civilians), and the ever more complex nature of the modern world, require a more coherent approach to our personnel policies, in order to maximise combat effectiveness. Our personnel strategy recognises that the ethos of each Service develops and adapts over time as traditions are subtly modified in light of experience. Service ethos is about cohesion within a structured chain of command, and is fundamental to enabling the Services to conduct operations.

We will continue to promote the Naval Service, the Army and the Royal Air Force as the individual components of the British Armed Forces.

Section 4 – The Future

Our Armed Forces have risen to the task of defending our Nation and our interests throughout history. Their determination, their commitment, their dedication and their service have defended and preserved our freedoms and traditions and the Nation's democracy and way of life.

Today our Service men and women, both regulars and reservists, have the same determination, the same commitment and the same dedication, and can be called upon to make the same sacrifice both now and in the future. To maintain these high standards in the future we aim to:

- Cultivate – 'prepare the ground' for obtaining personnel.
- Obtain – attract, acquire and train high quality, motivated people.
- Retain – provide personnel with a rewarding career which stimulates and develops them and provides the foundation of a second career on leaving the Services.
- Sustain – provide an environment in which Service men and women and their families will be willing to maintain their commitment.
- Remember – provide ex-Service personnel and their dependants with help and support, particularly with resettlement back into civilian life.

Our personnel must be well equipped for the tasks they are given and the demands on them and their families must not be unreasonable. We will recognise the special circumstances of Service families and address them wherever possible. We are determined to put in place modern and fair policies so that the Armed Forces attract and retain the right people and better reflect the society they serve – acknowledging, however, the need for the Armed Forces to be different in some areas.

We will address the issues of today and tomorrow. We have pledged ourselves to a continuous improvement in all our policies and practices so that they meet the needs of an ever changing world. We shall strive to achieve a balance of resources between platforms, weapons and people. The AFOPS will provide a coherent framework for taking forward people issues as we move into the 21st century.

'TOLERABLE VARIATION'

The development of the AFOPS has led to a clearer definition of the division of responsibilities in the formulation of Service personnel policy between the Centre and the single Services.

It is clear that even in the five years since Sir Michael Bett's Independent Review (IR)[1] was published, the role of the Centre in personnel policy has increased. In some of the Centre-led policy areas, there is little leeway in how policies are implemented by the single Services (e.g. equal opportunities, pay, and pensions). However, there are other Centre-led policy areas where the single Services vary, within agreed limits, the manner in which Centre prescribed policies are implemented; this will continue. This ability to vary is 'tolerable variation'. There are other areas where the Services are wholly responsible for the policy and its implementation. A clear understanding of the definition and application of 'tolerable variation' is required to support the application of the AFOPS.

Background

The IR described the concept of 'tolerable variation', as relating to employment conditions, as follows:[2]

> *'2.14 Some aspects of the employment package for Servicemen will necessarily be common to all three Services (for example, main features of the rank structure and pay structure, charges, certain allowances, leave and pension schemes). However, each Service carries out a different task, with different equipment, with differently trained manpower, with different skills. It would therefore be wrong and inefficient to try and force the three Services into the same mould for all their personnel policies.*
>
> *2.15 We therefore recommend that a prime task for the Service Personnel Board should be to develop an overall strategic personnel policy and then to ensure that each Service develops its own sub-strategy, policies and practices relevant to its own needs as they are foreseen and develop. This would mean determining which employment conditions needed to be common and which could differ, within a prescribed bandwidth of tolerable variation, according to the needs of each Service.'*

The IR contended that some aspects of the employment package should be common to all three Services, but that due to the differences between them, they should not be compelled into common personnel policies. The concept of 'prescribed bandwidth of tolerable variation' was its means of addressing this issue. The 'Armed Forces of the Future' Information Document³ introduced a 'Personnel Strategy' but was silent on 'tolerable variation'.

Definition of 'Tolerable Variation

Work on this subject produced three possible definitions for 'tolerable variation':

a. First, at the topmost level, 'tolerable variation' could be taken as applying to the division of responsibility for policy formulation between the Centre and the single Services. At this level, 'tolerable variation' would mean that in those policy areas set by themselves the single Services would have 'primacy'. This arrangement, though, is essentially a division of responsibility; it is not one in which a degree of variance is 'tolerated'.

b. Second, 'tolerable variation' could be taken as applying a level further down. At this lower level, 'tolerable variation' would mean that in some Centre-led areas policies would be set to apply only to one or two Services. In other words, it would be possible for some Centre-led policies not to apply to the other one or two Services *at all*. This definition is more in line with the IR contention. If this definition were accepted, we would be perpetuating the practice of Service personnel engaged in similar activities being treated differently.

c. Third, 'tolerable variation' could be taken as applying to Centre-led personnel policies which apply to two or more single Services, although elements of the *application* of the policies might vary in one or more Service.

The most rational and productive definition of 'tolerable variation' was that outlined at paragraph 'c' (above). Furthermore, where 'tolerable variation' was sought, a mechanism for identifying and demonstrating the need for it would be needed. In short, there was a need to set the principles under which 'tolerable variation' would apply.

It was not the wish or intention of the Central Staff to be overly prescriptive. It was acknowledged that each Service was different and has its own requirements. Furthermore, whilst the Central Staff (in consultation with the single Services) would set the policy; the single Services were and would remain responsible for its implementation.

Principles of 'Tolerable Variation'

In Centre-led areas, 'tolerable variation' should be allowed once a case has been demonstrated according to a set of agreed principles. Such demonstration should be against two series of principles. The first set would be 'mandatory', the second 'advisory' and not necessarily a bar to 'tolerable variation' if the evidence supporting the first set is sufficiently strong:

a. **Mandatory Principles.**

(1) Demonstration that the application of 'tolerable variation' is essential to the maintenance of single Service operational effectiveness.

(2) Demonstration that the application of 'tolerable variation' is a significant single Service recruitment or retention factor.

b. **Advisory Principles.**

(1) Demonstration that the application of 'tolerable variation' is coherent with the AFOPS and/or the single Service Personnel Strategy.

(2) Demonstration that the application of 'tolerable variation' would not be at odds with the trend towards increasingly joint operations.

(3) Demonstration that the application of 'tolerable variation' could be communicated to personnel of the other Services serving in the same location.

PROCEDURES

If one or more single Service feels that it has a case for 'tolerable variation', it should first decide whether it could demonstrate that the case meets the mandatory principles detailed above. In most cases initial discussions as to the merit of the proposal would take place in the appropriate Centre/single Service working forum formed under Centre leadership in the functional policy area. This would require good leadership, co-operation and compromise, with no individual Service having a veto. The principle of undertaking business at the lowest level would apply and, in most cases, it should be possible to agree minor 'tolerable variations' at this level and make recommendations on more significant 'tolerable variations' to 'One Star' level and above. Any agreements of significant 'tolerable variations' would have to be supported by casework which should contain demonstrable evidence to support the case and address the advisory principles. This casework would provide the basis for agreement with the Treasury, if required, and as the record of action for any future audit. It is anticipated that most 'tolerable variation' would be agreed as policy was formulated or reviewed in the normal course of business – there should be few cases where a single Service suddenly discovered it wished 'tolerable variation' on a well established policy.

REVIEW

The AFOPS will put us in a position to review our personnel policies. In so doing, it recognises that Britain's Defence depends on the personnel who serve in the Naval Service, the Army and the Royal Air Force and the civilians who work alongside them. It acknowledges that the Armed Forces' operational capability is founded upon the quality of its people and that the Armed Forces must recruit and retain their share of the best people the country has to offer from a diverse society. It offers a vision for Service men and women thus:

'To generate and maintain modern, joint, battle winning forces, by placing Service personnel and their families at the centre of our plans, investing in them and giving them confidence in their future.'

NOTES

1. Bett M. *Independent Review of the Armed Forces' Manpower, Career and Remuneration Structures: Managing People in Tomorrow's Armed Forces.* London, HMSO, 1995.
2. Ibid. pp. 11–12.
3. 'The Armed Forces of the Future: A Personnel Strategy' – An Information Document by the Ministry of Defence dated February 1997.

3

A Wasted Investment? The Career Management of Royal Signals Young Officers

GRAHAM COMPLIN
Royal Signals

INTRODUCTION

"Knowing why, when and how to change is key to maintaining an Army's effectiveness"[1]

In his paper *"Towards The Future Army"*,[2] Colonel Dick Applegate outlines his vision of where he believes the British Army is heading in the next century. His view empasises the Human Resource Management (HRM) aspect of future strategy development:

> *"...Its members will be highly motivated, with an ethos emphasising commitment, self sacrifice, mutual trust and the highest professional standards."*

The dilemma that the Army faces is that currently the realities of recruiting and retention bear little resemblance to the projected 'end state' of the full manning HR scenarios depicted by the likes of Colonel Applegate and the Chief of the General Staff, General Sir Roger Wheeler, whose *"Vision for the Army"*[3] includes the comment:

> *"A high quality professional Army, valued by the Nation, robust and useable; an Army ready to undertake at short notice any tasks required of it from civil aid to warfighting."*

As at 1st April 1999 there was an overall manning deficit of 8,854 personnel (310 officers, and 8,544 soldiers), with full manning not anticipated until at least 2005.

While it is apparent that the Army is becoming more proficient in attracting young men and women into the forces via effective recruitment policies, it is failing to retain sufficient numbers to achieve the full manning target.[5] Retention has been described by the Adjutant General as the *"Vital Ground"* for the Army.[6] This is hardly surprising when it costs six times more to recruit a soldier rather than retain one; it is estimated that it costs at least £35,000 to replace each Young Officer (YO) who decides to leave the Army prematurely.[7]

There has been some debate in the press, alluding to a *"mass exodus"* of officers who are disillusioned at the realities of *"the job failing to match the image"*.[8] While the data used in this particular report was later described as *"selective"* by the Defence Analytical Services Agency[9] (DASA), the perception remains that arguably the current career management of YO's is instrumental in compounding the retention problem.

This chapter seeks to establish a relationship, primarily utilising Peter Senge's work,[10] between current Royal Signals Young Officer career management, the career management and retention of soldiers and unit efficiency

CURRENT ROYAL SIGNALS YOUNG OFFICER CAREER MANAGEMENT

A commission in the Royal Signals arguably offers a unique challenge within the British Army. First and foremost its officers are expected to be dynamic leaders with the ability to motivate and command soldiers at all levels. Secondly, a high degree of technical expertise is demanded to ensure that the Corps' primary responsibility within the army for Command, Control, Communications Information Systems (CIS) and Electronic Warfare (EW) is maintained. With this balance in mind, the Corps now primarily recruits graduates with good officer qualities, who are capable of assimilating and putting into practice the technical aspects of the Royal Signals special to arm training they receive following attendance at the Royal Military Academy Sandhurst (RMAS). Indeed, over 80% of Royal Signals officer recruits are now graduates,[11] direct from civilian university, with an average age of 24.5. This should be compared to the average age of the Royal Signals Young Officer entrant in previous years of 21.5 years.[12]

This relatively significant increase in the age of its YOs has created a considerable career management challenge for the Corps, particularly with promotion to Major now being available at age 30.[13] On average 22% of Captains were promoted to Major at age 30 in 1997,[14] although this figure was reduced to 12% by 1998.[15] The implication is, however, that where possible an officer must be given the opportunity, having received only six annual Confidential Reports (CRs), to be eligible for promotion. This should be compared against officers who in previous years, had an average age of entry of 21.5 and could amass up to 11 reports before going into the promotion zone for the first time at 32.[16] Brigadier N F Wood, former Signal Officer in Chief (Army), even noted that:

"In some cases newly commissioned [Royal Signals] *officers are coming out of Sandhurst as late as 26 or even 27 years of age, thereby reducing the length of time available for regimental experience."*[17]

The problem that the Corps faces is that in order to produce a career profile that will allow YOs to compete for promotion at age 30,[18] it has developed a career management policy that moves personnel through regimental duty posts quickly and appoints them to key regimental staff appointments, such as Adjutant, earlier. Figure 1 (p.32) outlines how a YO's early career could develop. This manning policy effectively contradicts the role of the YO as outlined in the Royal Signals prospectus, the Corps' primary recruiting document. Here, the role of the YO is described as:

"Your job at each rank as an officer, will be firstly to weld them [soldiers] *into a strong team and then to deploy them with utter confidence when playing for the very highest stakes. In turn, these soldiers will expect their officers always to give them purposeful direction and support in all their work, to supervise their individual professional and military training, and to provide them with advice concerning their careers."*[19]

It can be argued that the current YO career management policy undermines the retention of not only officer entrants but also soldiers. HQ Land Command noted that there is a leadership issue at stake:

> "... *At the platoon/troop level the preponderance of graduate officers increases the emphasis on 'career' at the expense of leadership and command.*"[21]

FIGURE 1
CURRENT ROYAL SIGNALS "IDEAL CAREER PATTERN"
FOR YOUNG OFFICERS

Ser	Age	Appointment	Remarks
1	24.5–26.5	Troop Commander	Possibly two short tours of one year[20] (following RMAS and special to arm training).
2	26.5–28	Squadron Second in Command	New unit
3	28.5	Attendance at Junior Command and Staff Course (JCSC) – 17 week "Captains' Course"	Ideally between postings
4	28.5–30	Adjutant/Regimental Operations Officer	New unit
5	30–34	Staff College/Sub-Unit Command/ Grade 3 staff appointment.	

Source: Dryburgh J. (former SO2 Offrs R SIGNALS), "The Junior Officer's 'Truncated Career'", *The Wire.* Vol.51 No.5, p.41.

Brigadier J H Griffin, Signal Officer in Chief (Army) described this situation as the *"Phantom Young Officer"* syndrome. He further added:

> "*The principal role of officers is to train their soldiers and lead them on operations. I am sure that we are currently going out of our way to produce the most broadly trained officer we can and then leaving him or her no time to put this learning into practice with soldiers, what they are paid to do. **This is at least a wasted investment, at worst a dereliction of duty and I have no doubt that it contributes to our current parlous retention situation.**"*[22]

It is within the context of the current challenging manning climate that it is appropriate to consider the career management and development of Royal Signals YOs from a holistic HRM perspective.

The Problem: Learning Disabilities.

Senge advocates that there are primarily six *"Learning Disabilities"* as a direct result of *"Linear Thinkers"* seeing and thinking in straight lines as opposed to *"System Thinkers"* who perceive that everyone shares responsibility for problems generated by a system.[23] In relation to career management and development the following *"Learning Disabilities"* have relevance:[24]

- **Delusion of Learning from Experience.** We may learn best from experiences, but people often never experience the consequences of many of their most important decisions.

  Certainly current Royal Signals YO Career Management policy advocates that *"Experience"* is an essential feature of personnel development. The Corps fails however to ensure that longevity complements this policy, thus creating Senge's delusion of learning from experience.

- **I Am My Position.** While people understand their daily tasks, they do not understand the purpose of the enterprises they take part in.

  This is arguably the case of the current generation of YO Troop Commanders. Is the appointment just another part of their career portfolio, which must be completed prior to advancement, or is it an opportunity to effectively lead and manage soldiers in order to maximise retention? The following statement, made by a 23-year-old male Royal Signals YO, during the attitude survey for this chapter suggests that the former may exist amongst some:

"Graduate officers on the whole no longer see the position of Troop Commander as an important one. They see it merely as a stepping stone to better things."

The Army produces a lot of "vision statements" – The Army HR Strategy, which aspires to achieve full manning by 2005, is a particularly worthy one. Retention is the cornerstone of this strategy and therefore the domain of all serving personnel. My analysis will show that the *"HR-Vision"* has not percolated down to the majority of service personnel so the opportunity to foster spirit and commitment is wasted.

- **Team Learning.** Senge proposes that *"Team Learning"* is vital because teams, not individuals are the fundamental learning unit in modern organisations. The discipline of team learning starts with 'dialogue', the ability to enter into a genuine *"thinking together"*. Additionally it is essential to have the capacity to recognise the patterns of interaction in teams that undermine learning.

   This aspect of Senge's thesis reads remarkably like the characteristics required of YOs when serving as Troop Commanders. Their position as the Team Leader is pivotal in developing *"Team Learning"*, which is as Senge points out *"where the rubber hits the road"*; for unless teams can learn, the organisation cannot learn.

Peter Senge offers some useful organisational theories, which could be effectively utilised in evaluating and improving current practices. His thesis is founded on the brave assumption that traditional top-down management has had its day. One could argue, therefore that his subsequent initiatives have no place in the British Army, which is very much a hierarchical and linear organisation. However, the concept of *"Mission Command"*,[25] which devolves responsibility away from the centre, indicates that there is a relatively high degree of autonomy already within the Army and it might therefore benefit by evaluating Senge's initiatives.

   It is intended to develop one of Peter Senge's models from his book *"The Fifth Discipline"*. The model in question, illustrated in Figure 2, is entitled *"Fixes That Fail"* and is described as:

> *"A fix, effective in the short term, has unforeseen long-term consequences which may require even more use of the same fix."*[26]

This model has been significantly developed by Lieutenant Colonel William Bell of the US Army. His original paper was entitled *"The Impact of Policies on Organizational Values and Culture"*[27] and was written for the Joint Services Commission

FIGURE 2
FIXES THAT FAIL

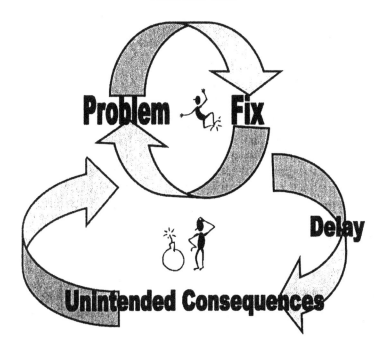

Source: Senge PM. *The Fifth Discipline*, pp. 388–9.

on Professional Ethics. It discusses the concept that all policies have unintended 2nd and 3rd order consequences or side effects that take significant time to come to the attention of senior leadership. He argued that these effects could either be positive or negative and that it is in the 2nd and 3rd order effects that the problems occur with most policies. This is because:

- They are difficult to anticipate.
- They can interact in unforeseeable ways.
- Their effects can slowly build over time.
- When detected their interpretation can be discounted or biased due to overconfidence or organisational compartmentalisation.

Succinctly he added:

> *"For the individual, the intended effects of policies are meaningless; only the actual effects of policies on the individuals have meaning. It is what impacts the individual that determines his behaviour as well as his understanding of the actual organisational values system."*[28]

The Unintended Consequences of YO Career Management.

Bell argued that if the actual effects of policies on individuals are left uncorrected over a sufficiently long time, these unintended consequences of Army Policies could change Army culture in ways the Army did not intend.[29] For the purpose of this chapter it is proposed to illustrate that through the current policy of YO Career Management (**1st Order Effect**) the unintended consequences are:

- **2nd Order Effect** – Soldier Career Management and Retention.
- **3rd Order Effect** – Unit Efficiency.

THE EFFECTS OF CURRENT CAREER MANAGEMENT POLICIES ON YOUNG OFFICERS – THE 1ST ORDER EFFECT

It is generally acknowledged from within the Army that current officer career management policy is flawed; particularly during the formative stages. The Officer Recruitment Working Group (ORWG) recently identified the following key issues in this area:[30]

- Career compression during the first 8 years of service has a profound psychological effect on YOs and is a significant and negative influence on recruiting and retention.

- YOs do not have enough time to acquire vital professional experience, learn from their mistakes and achieve optimum performance. This impacts significantly on job satisfaction.

- YOs expect early responsibility and the opportunity to lead. Their first command is a pivotal experience, and for many is too short, dislocating expectations.

Additionally it has been recognised that career compression is widely acknowledged as one of the root causes of dissatisfaction and outflow from the Army. The Premature Volunteer Release (PVR) rate for junior officers aged 26–30 has risen from 89 per annum in 1995 to 138 in 1998 and continues to rise.[31] The reasons for this increase are varied but it is of note that the *Officer's Leaver Survey* highlights career compression as one of the top six most important reasons for officer's electing to leave.[32] The aim of this chapter is therefore not to necessarily demonstrate that the current YO career management system is flawed, as this fact appears to be beyond dispute, but rather to focus on its effects, both culturally and professionally on Royal Signals YOs.

Serve to Lead?

Much of the data for this chapter was based upon primary research involving a combination of field work, interviews with senior Royal Signals officers (2 Brigadiers and 5 Commanding Officers) and a survey that was sent to 150 Royal Signals Young Officers with less than five years commissioned service. The aim of the survey, designed using Oppenheim's *"Quintamensional Plan"*,[33] was to gauge attitudes to career management and related issues. It resulted in a 60%-plus response; thus providing a representative and usable source of information.

It would be useful to begin the analysis of the results of this research with a reminder of the purpose of officer training at the Royal Military Academy Sandhurst (motto: *Serve to Lead*). The aim of the RMAS course is:

> *"To develop the qualities of leadership and to provide the basic knowledge required by all young officers of any Arms or Service so that after the necessary specialist training appropriate to that Arm or Service they will be fit to be junior commanders."*[34]

The ethos of the course is founded on nurturing leadership skills in cadets to enable them to ultimately lead the soldiers under their command by example. The Commandant, Major General Arthur Denaro, believes that the current generation of officer cadets are older, more mature and more questioning than ever; a fact in his opinion that 85% of students are now graduates as opposed to 40% five or six years ago.[35] It is of little surprise, therefore, that on commissioning YOs are conditioned to expect command of soldiers and the opportunity to demonstrate the leadership skills that they have recently acquired. Even in a technical corps such as the Royal Signals, early command opportunities play a large part in influencing a YO's cap-badge selection. This concept was demonstrated in the Attitude Survey when over 75% of respondents agreed with the statement that early career leadership opportunities and command of soldiers were key factors in selecting the Royal Signals as their cap-badge.

It is not difficult to sympathise with YOs, therefore, when after approximately two years troop commanding they discover that what they perceive to be their primary function and role – *command and leadership* – is to be replaced with a succession of desk-bound appointments. This is clearly demonstrated in the survey when nearly 70% of respondents stated that they were disillusioned by the shortage of time spent in command of soldiers. Of additional concern is that the survey illustrated that on average a YO is likely to undertake two separate appointments during the two years spent in command in order to afford them the breadth of experience that the Corps considers necessary (the most extreme example from the survey indicated that a subaltern had commanded five separate troops in two different units during a two-year period as a Troop Commander). This policy is over-whelmingly opposed by YOs. Over 85% of respondents considered that the frequent transition of officers through troops to be detrimental to the management and welfare of soldiers, while over 60% considered the policy as damaging to unit efficiency. Brigadier Hughes, Commander 2 (National Communications) Signal Brigade, however, supported the policy of broad experience. He argued that in peacetime the onus should be biased towards developing the individual officer and accepting the resultant compromise to unit efficiency. During the Transition to War (TTW) he considered that the balance should shift to the "*Organisation*" with YOs "*bonding*" with their troops during pre-deployment training.[36] In contrast, all of the Commanding Officers interviewed challenged this policy and argued for "*quality*" YO appointments rather than "*quantity*". The current climate of high operational tempo[37] further compounded the problem as the policy of deploying Individual Reinforcements (IRs) on operations rather than formed sub-units was damaging cohesion and morale.[38]

Serve for Me?

Arguably, the present career management process has created a generation of officers who have become quickly disillusioned with the realities of their environment which has subsequently forced them to adjust their goals and values in order to conform and progress. Certainly there is a perception amongst senior officers that the current career management process, is *"Individual rather than structure orientated"*,[39] and has created a culture of *"ticket punching"*[40] amongst YOs. Some senior officers such as Lieutenant Colonel Couch regard this group as a *"vocal minority"* who do not represent the majority of YOs.[41] He did concede, however, that he sensed that YOs generally were *"impatient for progress"*. Lieutenant Colonel Lithgow attributed this *"will to succeed"* culture to the three phases of redundancy in the early 1990s which effectively destroyed the previous *"job for life"* mentality that existed. In his view the reason why the current generation of YOs are so keen to advance is in order to gain a Regular Commission, (which now has to be gained through recommendations and in competition with fellow officers as opposed to previously being granted on commissioning) so that *they* and not the Army can decide when it was time to leave the service.[42] Lieutenant Colonel Terrington commented that more than ever YOs are arguably too aware of their career milestones and the fear of failure amongst Troop Commanders to avoid mistakes and *"career foul"* is significant.[43] Interestingly, Lieutenant Colonel Couch contested this notion with the view that if there is undue pressure on YOs to succeed then it is primarily the fault of the Commanding Officer rather than the system. He argued that it is within the gift of the Commanding Officer to diffuse this tension amongst his or her YOs.[44]

Conversely, Brigadier Cook, Commander 11th Signal Brigade, questioned whether awareness of one's career milestones was necessarily a retrograde step. In his view, just because a previous generation did not (overtly) concern themselves with such matters does not demonstrate a failing on the part of today's YOs for choosing to focus on it.[45] It is of note that while the majority of YOs are disillusioned by the shortage of time spent in command, only approximately 30% consider that they spent an inadequate period of time as a Troop Commander. With hindsight, this survey question highlighted an issue that many YOs could not answer. At what stage do officers know if they have spent an appropriate amount of time as a Troop Commander? Certainly the overwhelming majority (80%) do not feel that they were in any way misled by the Royal Signals Recruiting Staff over how much time they would spend in command. There does appear to be a dichotomy, however, between the intuitive feeling that the period spent as a Troop Commander is too disjointed and brief and the realisation and acceptance that promotion and progression is linked to a portfolio of primarily non-command appointments.

By creating and managing career compression the British Army has arguably developed an officer corps that is primarily focused on achieving early promotion through the successful completion of a number of predominantly administrative appointments without the benefit of adequate tactical experience.[46] Bernard Roskter, a noted US HRM expert, described a similar situation in the US Army as:

> "High billet throughput lowers the quality of tour experiences. The "dash for the top"... has resulted in limiting opportunities for officers to fully develop needed proficiencies by trying to do too much in too little time...In order to position top candidates for upper military leadership positions, individuals often serve for a limited time in certain assignments to satisfy necessary career milestones. While high billet throughput may afford some individuals a broadened experience base, true expertise and competence cannot be achieved except for only basic or elementary tasks."[47]

Brigadier Hughes contests the idea that the career management process has contributed to raising individuals' level of expectation to the point where it has become their primary motivating factor.[48] However, in his 1990 book *Inside The British Army* Antony Beevor notes that senior officers are *"flabbergasted"* when YOs:

"Stroll up and ask about their best career move....we never gave a thought to that sort of thing at least not until we were in line for Staff College"[49]

This mindset is attributable, in my view, to the disjointed response to the survey question regarding suitability for more senior appointments. While 60% of YOs were willing to concede that more time spent as a Troop Commander would be beneficial to their own career development, only 25% of respondents indicated that they disagreed with the notion that the short period of time spent in command had left them ill equipped and short of the experience required for more senior regimental appointments. This seeming contradiction could either be as a result of pride, self-confidence or a genuine reluctance to acknowledge personal shortcomings in a career structure where early responsibility is the norm rather than the exception.

Lieutenant Colonel Terrington considered that as a direct result of career compression, particularly at Regimental Duty (RD), YOs were consequently failing to benefit from the additional professional development that was afforded to their predecessors. On the Job Training (OJT), in his view, was pivotal to the education of YOs, both from a technical perspective and to serve to reinforce the practicalities of leadership and man-management. As a Commanding Officer he viewed the limited amount of time a YO spends as a Troop Commander as a *"window of opportunity"* for him to give them as much training as possible in an attempt to compensate for the effects of career compression on their professional development. Consequently, he placed great emphasis on Study Days[50] as a method of balancing lost experience.[51] This policy appeared to be the norm at all the regiments visited during my research. Lieutenant Colonel Couch did make the point, however that *"Training can not substitute for lost experience."*[52]

In my view the officer corps has arguably drifted from a *"Serve to Lead"* ethos to a *"Serve for Me"* culture, partly as a result of the career management structure. This is primarily because officer career management is viewed very much as a separate entity, as opposed to utilising a more systemic approach that considers all of the dynamic factors involved in the overall efficiency of the organisation.[53] Segal and Sinaiko refer to this culture as *"Careerist"* and *"Opportunist"*. They argue that these sub-cultures exist within the British Army and are populated by those concerned primarily with the personal benefits and advantages that are to be gained from military service.[54] Antony Beever reinforces this notion with a quote from a subaltern from the Foot Guards: *"We're now thinking ten years ahead and worrying ten years ahead."*[55]

It is acknowledged that career management is not the only factor contributing to this culture. In *Inside The British Army* Antony Beevor discusses the new generation of *"Thatcher"* YOs who are *"no longer beguiled by the eccentricities and are far more interested in their 'conditions of service', in other words their perks."*[56] More recently the Bett Report highlighted the fundamental social and cultural changes that now impact on the Services. Bett contested that young people now expect more from their employment: stability, career development and future employability (rather than specific job security); more autonomy in their work and greater intellectual challenge.[57] It could be concluded, therefore that current career management policy has compounded rather than rectified the *"Me Generation"* that the Army now primarily recruits from. One senses that it is important to keep this issue in perspective. The officer corps remains an attractive career option and continues to recruit high-quality motivated individuals with a genuine desire to lead and serve. Both Lieutenant Colonel Lithgow and Lieutenant Colonel Couch emphasised the quality and high standard of education of their YOs. Lieutenant Colonel Couch's primary concern was with the current compressed career structure as opposed to the current generation of YOs,[58] whereas Lieutenant Colonel Lithgow was critical of the limited employability of YOs.[59] The survey indicated that the overwhelming majority (80%) recognised the shortcomings of the current career structure and expressed a desire to be part of a process that allowed them to gain more experience during the early stages of their career.

In his book *The Soldier in Modern Society*, Baynes argues that the *"modern"* Army officer should be a combination of both a *"hero"* and a *"manager"*; he used the term *"site boss"* as perhaps the best non-military description.[60] Although Baynes's book is a rather dated view on the *modus operandi* and culture of the Army in the 1960s it does serve to illustrate the traditional role of the YO that I believe we have strayed from. Arguably the current generation of YOs fail to fully reflect either the *"hero"* or *"manager"* role. Antony Beevor quotes one Commanding Officer:

> *"A platoon's probably the best command they'll ever have but they just don't believe me when I tell them that. They're too impatient, that's why they've got so little commitment. If things aren't working fast enough for them, then they'll be off. The graduates first of all."*[61]

As previously discussed, officer career management policy does not just impact on the officer corps. There are other unintended consequences; namely issues regarding soldier management and unit efficiency (the 2nd and 3rd order effects).

SOLDIER MANAGEMENT – THE 2ND ORDER EFFECT

In his paper "Ethos: British Army Officership 1962–1992" Patrick Mileham offers his view on the relationship between officers and soldiers in the modern British Army:

> *"While Lord Moran could say confidently (in 1945) of the Great War British soldier 'the soldier is governed through his heart and not his head' such is now not the character of the modern British soldier. His understanding is well developed, and unless his leaders impress him that orders are intelligent and the work of the Army is conducted in a thoroughly professional manner and objective way, the soldier will not put his heart into it."*[62]

The British Army has long prided itself on the Regimental System, which emphasises human bonding. Experience shows that people do their upmost in war for fear of letting down their colleagues, rather than for the more obscure reasons of country, county or town.[63] It is therefore necessary to create in peace and war the basis for this comradeship. The Regimental System seeks to foster this *esprit de corps*, aided at all levels by effective leadership. Arguably, one of the most critical links in the leadership chain is the YO who is at the *"coal-face"* of the officer corps, and who invariably acts as the direct interface to the non-commissioned ranks without whose support the Regimental System is worthless. Effective leadership at this level is pivotal to creating and maintaining the *esprit de corps* that has proved so vital to success in the past. It would therefore be appropriate to consider the effectiveness of YOs in their role of Troop Commander from a soldier's perspective.

Royal Signals Soldier Management

In 1996, Major P Kelly Royal Signals conducted a study entitled "Why are Soldiers Leaving the Royal Signals Prematurely?"[64] His study involved visiting nine units and interviewing some 317 Royal Signals soldiers and applying the concepts of Fredrick Herzberg[65] to examine the motivation to work, and in looking at the impact of extrinsic factors on role satisfaction and dissatisfaction.[66]

His main conclusions were that the primary causes of dissatisfaction amongst soldiers arose from an absence of intrinsic rewards within the job, and that this resulted from, in the main:

- Poor man management.

- Lack of information.

- Career mis-management.

- Lack of trust.

- Inconsistencies in the treatment of soldiers.

- An inadequate relationship with officers.

These conclusions resulted from a survey of soldiers, which produced the indicators regarding the current officer/soldier relationship illustrated in Figure 3.

Major Kelly's findings appear to reinforce the notion that Troop Commanders are currently not being given the opportunity to maximise their relationship with soldiers and provide a level of career management for them that is arguably missing at present. In my view this is primarily due to:

44

FIGURE 3
WHY ARE SOLDIERS LEAVING THE ROYAL SIGNALS PREMATURELY?

Statement	Disagree/Agree
Young officers are more concerned with their careers than looking after me.	62% Agree
My career is handled well.	75.4% Disagree
My Troop Officer provides good leadership	53.6% Disagree
The Corps cares about me	81.6% Disagree
Your life in the Corps has met your expectations.	69.3% Disagree

Source: Major P M Kelly Royal Signals. *Why are Soldiers Leaving the Royal Signals Prematurely?* Presentation to the Signal Officer in Chief (Army), 16th December 1996.

- A succession of quick-fire appointments which ensure that a YO is not given the opportunity to immerse him or herself in the ethos of troop life and earn the confidence of their soldiers.

- A lack of core management training that would enable YOs to provide effective *"first line"* career management guidance to their soldiers.

- An ill-defined corporate soldier career management policy.

Young Officer Employment Policy

The first element of this trilogy of soldier management concerns has previously been identified and discussed in some detail. It is of note, however, that the YO Attitude Survey carried out as part of this study revealed that over 80% of respondents indicated that more time spent as a Troop Commander would be beneficial to the management and retention of Royal Signals soldiers. There must be a conscious move away from moving YOs around (and within) units in order to give them *"experience."* It is of note that the survey indicated that a YO is likely to have on average **two separate appointments** (either within the same unit or elsewhere) during his or her two year employment as a Troop Commander. A balance needs to be struck between developing the individual and providing effective and meaningful leadership for soldiers. It is acknowledged that the Signal Officer in Chief (Army) has previously requested Commanding Officers to avoid moving YOs *"for the sake of experience"*[67] but the survey indicates that this practice is continuing.

Young Officer Management Training

The survey for this chapter indicated that over 90% of respondents considered that the Troop Commander has a key role to play in the career management and retention of soldiers. It would be worth considering, therefore, if the Royal Signals prepare them adequately for what is a pivotal function.

Analysis of the Royal Signals Troop Commanders Course Syllabus[68] indicates that of an 18-week course[69] the following *"Career Management"* subjects are covered:

- Mock Promotion Board – 4 periods.

- Career Management *'multi-choice test'* – 1 period.

- Introduction to the Army Welfare Service – 4 periods.

- Royal Signals Manning and Career Management Division – 3 periods.

The focus of the Troop Commanders course is primarily technical training; rightly so in my opinion, given the role and function of the Royal Signals. It is arguable, however, that insufficient emphasis has been placed on soldier career management; a significant failing by the Corps according to Lieutenant Colonel Lithgow, Commanding Officer 30 Signal Regiment.[70] The 1996 *"Job Analysis of the Royal Signals Troop Commander"* carried out by the Royal Signals Training Development Team (TDT) acknowledged that the current generation of Troop Commanders find key aspects of soldier career management *"relatively difficult, as well as important."*[71] Interestingly, the same report indicated that one of the main distastes experienced by Troop Commanders was *"Becoming involved with the personal problems of Troop personnel."*[72] This mindset could be attributable to the lack of emphasis placed on man-management on the Troop Commanders course or reflect the Peter Senge *"I am my Position"* culture as previously discussed.

More recently Headquarters Royal Signals has acknowledged that recognised linkage between increased management training and the retention challenge. A 1997 scoping paper[73] on the subject identified that the trends of modern society are being imported into the Army. These are placing greater demands on leaders and requiring a dynamic relationship with management skills. The trends identified were:

- More intelligent, better informed and more questioning subordinates. As a consequence they are less biddable. Those in the chain of command will therefore have to place greater emphasis on reasoned argument and persuasion rather than compulsion.

- A more materialistic society that finds itself at odds with the ethos of the service.

- Expectations are more commercial than vocational.

- Individual rights are not related to accompanying obligations.

Consequently it was recognised that in particular Troop Commanders would benefit from a course that enabled them to acquire management skills.[74] In 1997 Colonel C L Le Galalis OBE, Commander Royal School of Signals acknowledged that the current Troop Commanders course places too much emphasis on the *"Physical"* rather than the *"Moral"* domain of *"Fighting Power"*.[75] Although there has been no subsequent change to the Troop Commanders course syllabus as yet, I was advised by Brigadier Griffin, the Signal Officer in Chief (Army), that the programme was currently being re-written to reflect a requirement for a formal management module.[76]

Formalising the Young Officer's Role in Soldier Career Management

There appears to be something of a dichotomy over the issue of responsibility for soldier career management, which could be partly attributable to soldiers' general dissatisfaction in this area. The Army Continuous Attitude Survey identifies career development as one of the primary shortcomings by leavers while citing the same factor as one of the most important aspects of an Army career.[77] In my view general dissatisfaction in soldier career management is, in part, due to the relationship between Manning and Career Management Division (MCM Div) and units regarding *"ownership"* of soldiers' careers. By way of illustration, Major Wallis, SO2 Officers Royal Signals MCM Div contests (rightly in my view) that overarching soldier career management is the primary responsibility of his Headquarters.[78] In his opinion, as MCM Div has the only corporate view of Royal Signals manning and career issues, it is therefore best placed to promote, post, counsel and provide career courses for its personnel; a view endorsed by Lieutenant Colonel Canham, Commanding Officer, 11 Signal Regiment.[79]

Conversely the view from some commanding officers is (not unnaturally) somewhat different. For example, Lieutenant Colonel Terringtom, Commanding Officer 21st Signal Regiment (Air Support), made the valid point that soldier career management should be primarily the responsibility of units as they know soldiers as individuals rather than the contents of a personnel file. In his view MCM Div were essentially the *"executors"* who posted, promoted or otherwise managed personnel on the advice of commanding officers.[80]

In my opinion, the somewhat *"adversarial"* relationship between MCM Div and units regarding soldier career management has been borne by the lack of a formalised policy in this matter. The relationship, both intra-unit and between units and MCM (Div) should be agreed, with specific responsibility for the various elements and levels of soldier career management articulated so that conflict can be avoided.[81] The Troop Commander clearly has the potential to play a pivotal role in this area and should be regarded as the first port of call for any soldier career-management matters. Not only is the Troop Commander the most *"accessible"* officer to the majority of personnel but also occupies a key position to provide additional advice and recommendations up the chain of command. If it can be demonstrated to soldiers that the Troop Commander is supported by a structure that quickly and accurately provides the information required then there is scope to make a positive impact on current levels of dissatisfaction in this area.

This element of the chapter has sought to identify the impact of YO career management policy on soldiers. It was firstly demonstrated, primarily through the work of Major Kelly, that overall there is a high level of dissatisfaction with the performance of Troop Commanders among Royal Signals soldiers. Analysis has attributed this to the rapid transition of YOs through command appointments, the lack of quality soldier career management training and a disjointed and often adversarial relationship between units and MCM Div. Although the latter is not primarily the domain of YO career management it does imply that there is currently a *"missing link"* between the soldier, regimental headquarters and MCM Div that could be positively exploited.

UNIT EFFICIENCY – THE 3RD ORDER EFFECT

The measurement of unit efficiency and its relationship to career management policy is extremely subjective. Brigadier Cook, Commander 11 Signal Brigade, summed this up nicely by paraphrasing Peter Drucker thus: *"You can count the things that measure but you can't measure the things that count."*[82]

The *Measurement of Fighting Power* (MFP) is defined as an *"Army's capability to fight"* There are three interrelated components; the *conceptual* (the thought process), the *moral* (the ability to get people to fight) and the *physical* means (the means, equivalent to *'combat power'*).[83] While the physical means can be measured and the conceptual process refined through doctrine the moral component is difficult to define, let alone measure. The *British Military Doctrine* quotes Clausewitz on the subject:

"With uncertainty in one scale, courage and self-confidence must be thrown into the other to correct the balance."[84]

Additionally, the *British Military Doctrine* identifies the following elements of the Moral Component:[85]

- **High Morale**. This stems from sound training, confidence in commanders and equipment, discipline, clear

knowledge of what is going on and good administration.
* **Motivation.** The job of the commander is to instill purpose and create *esprit de corps*.
* **Leadership.** No military leader will succeed if he does not know the organisation, however large or small, that he is privileged to command.
* **Management.** Management skills are essential in the efficient running of an organisation and involve making the best use of resources.

It is clear that to judge the Moral Component of Fighting Power is largely an intuitive process.[86] It is such a grey area, according to Brigadier Cook, that it is hardly worth measuring. He is of the view that the factors that contribute to the moral component are so dynamic and variable that the whole issue is in a constant state of change.[87] It is therefore difficult to state; apart from intuitively, that current YO career management policy has a detrimental effect on the Moral Component of Fighting Power and *ergo* unit efficiency. The majority of senior officers interviewed agreed with this notion and one or two offered examples. Brigadier Hughes acknowledged that the rapid transition of YOs through troops probably impacted on the level of collective training and expertise that could ever be reached[88] while Lieutenant Colonel Terrington identified a relationship between the frequent movement of YOs through troops and a negative impact on soldiers' morale.[89] What is apparent from Major Kelly's study is that Royal Signals soldiers do not feel well led at troop level, while my survey indicated that the majority of YOs themselves (60%) feel that the frequent transition through units in order to gain experience is detrimental to unit efficiency. Furthermore, an increased majority (85%) of YOs consider that more time spent as a Troop Commander would be beneficial to unit efficiency.

In my view the current YO career management policy does not encourage the vision espoused by Colonel Dick Applegate at the beginning of this section. Morale of both soldiers and officers is suffering as a result of a structure that seeks to minimise the impact and influence of Troop Commanders on soldiers. This is primarily because officer career management is viewed as a separate entity and as a result erodes the constituent elements of the Moral

Component of Fighting Power; Morale, Leadership, Management and Motivation. All the *"things that count but cannot be measured"* can be directly and positively influenced by a YO; in my view they are not being given a chance under the present career structure.

ANALYSIS OF AN ALTERNATIVE CAREER MANAGEMENT MODEL – THE US ARMY

In order to provide a balanced overview of the British Army's YO career management system it would be useful to study a different organisation's process as a comparative model. The US Army was primarily selected for this purpose as it shares a similar ethos and culture to the British Army and therefore demands similar HRM requirements.[90] To ensure a balanced and more realistic appraisal of US policy, the author visited US Personnel Command (PERSCOM) in Washington DC where he interviewed Colonel Charles R. Scott, the Branch Chief of the US Signals Corps Personnel Branch. A visit to Fort Bragg in North Carolina was also undertaken where a Focus Group with US Army YOs from the 3rd Special Forces Battalion was carried out.

Experience – The Underpinning Principle of US Army Career Management

The key difference between the US and British Army system of career management is that the US calculate an officer's seniority for promotion dependent upon his or her *"Years of Service"* as opposed to the British system that uses *"Year of Birth"* as the key criterion. Figure 4 illustrates the minimum *"Time in Group" (TIG)* requirements for promotion to the next higher rank in the US Army. The *"Years of Service"* system is based on the entire US Officer Corps being graduates but with no antedated seniority.[91] Therefore, regardless of age, each officer will serve the prescribed time in each rank before becoming eligible for promotion. Age is not an issue in the US Army. Regulations prohibit promotion boards from knowing the age of officers being considered for promotion; the Year of Birth is blanked out of an officer's record during the promotion process.[92] The resultant effect of this policy is that US Army Commanding Officers could be significantly older than their British Army counterparts, given that officers can be commissioned up to the age of 33 in the US. Unlike the British Army, however, this is not generally considered to be detrimental to either the individual or the system. The emphasis in the US Army is much more *"Fitness for Role"* rather than age orientated. As long as an officer remains fit and passes his or her annual physical assessment then they are considered as potential commanders. It was conceded, however, by Colonel Scott that whilst the US Army is not *'ageist'*, an *'old looking'* 49-year-old Lieutenant Colonel might have some difficulty in obtaining a command appointment.[93]

FIGURE 4
US ARMY – OFFICER PROMOTION MILESTONES

Promote to	Years of Service
1LT	18 months
Captain	4 years[94]
Major	10 Years (+/– 1 year)
Lieutenant Colonel	16 Years (+/– 1 year)

Source: Commissioned Officer Development PAM 600-3

Interestingly the apparent frustrations in the British Army at the lack of early promotion that the *"Year of Birth"* system appears to create is not an obvious issue in the US Army. The UK view is epitomised in the following quote from the Continuous Attitude Survey:[95]

" *A career and promotion structure that is based on age (until the age of 37) is frustrating for someone who is ambitious and aged 29. (Captain)"*

The US Army culture of promotion through time and experience is widely accepted and has not been seriously challenged to date.[96] Arguably however, in order to counter any feeling of frustration the US Army is a keen practitioner of providing responsibility early. Unlike the British Army, however, it is not promotion-based. Instead, for example, companies and squadrons are commanded by Captains[97] rather than Majors, as is the case in Britain. Based on my personal experiences during the field trip one senses that the US Army embraces John F. Kennedy's vision to *"... ask not what your country can do for you – ask what you can do for your country."*[98]

Ultimately this could mean that many more of its officers elect to join the Army for more vocational reasons and therefore view a military career in a more selfless light than their British counterparts. This perception was reinforced during a Focus Group held at Fort Bragg, North Carolina with three YOs of the US Special Forces.[99] During the session there was no real criticism of the US Army career management and promotion structure, less the acknowledgement that the system was orientated primarily towards officer career development without necessarily considering the interests of the soldier or unit efficiency. This point was made following discussion regarding the potentially destabilising effect of Platoon Leaders and Company Commanders regularly rotating, potentially on an annual basis. The emphasis on formative experience[100] was acknowledged to be an important grounding for future command and staff appointments and there were no apparent frustrations with a system that rigidly promoted its officers relative to their length of service.[101]

The Evolution of US Army Officer Career Management

In 1995 the Army Deputy Chief of Staff for Personnel identified that the Officer Personnel Management System (OPMS) was in need of review, following concerns raised about leader development and assignment (posting) management.[102] Prior to this it had been noted that faced with a growing list of assignment requirements that competed directly with troop assignments, the amount of time spent in tactical units was being diminished. A recent US Army Report described tactical units as where:

> *"Young officers enhance their leadership and interpersonal skills, develop their tactical intuition, and gain confidence in being able to respond to challenging situations. They also acquire the confidence and competence required for more complex and higher level assignments."*[103]

The reduction in tactical assignments was attributed to a

number of factors. Some include congressionally mandated requirements such as assignments to joint positions or Reserve Component units. Others are related to the disproportionate reduction in tactical units in the US Army compared to non-troop unit organisations as part of the downsizing that followed the end of the Cold War. The net effect was by described in a US Army Paper as:

> *"A reduction in troop unit experience for future battalion and brigade commanders and a corresponding reduction in the development of key leadership and tactical skills."*[104]

Analysis of the actual impact of reduced troop assignments on leadership and tactical ability is largely subjective and difficult to quantify. However, it has been noted that in recent years the performance of both brigade commanders and entire combat teams at the various US Army's Combat Training Centres has experienced a downward trend. Lieutenant Colonel John Rosenburger, a former senior Observer/ Controller at the National Training Centre, believes that *"Leader Deficiency"* in the art of battle is the primary reason for this.[105]

The resultant review of the Officer Personnel Management System, entitled *OPMS XXI*, recognised that:

> *"Army systems depend on the skill and heart of the soldiers who use them, and officers play a critical role in the combined integration, synchronization, and employment of those soldiers and the systems they employ. High standards of performance- both individual officer skill and collective organisational skill – are required to maximise organisational performance. Therefore, officers must be given adequate time, education and developmental experience as individuals to become outstanding leaders."*[106]

This statement certainly embraces the holistic and strategic approach to HRM that General Reimer had advocated prior to the study. The linkage between officer development, soldier management and unit efficiency is clearly established and thereafter acted as a guiding principle for the report's various recommendations.

The "Muddy Boots" Culture

Having identified officer development as pivotal to the effectiveness of the Army, OPMS XXI discusses the importance of training Young Officers through a series of tactical unit assignments, thus ensuring that they embrace the *"Muddy Boots"* heritage of US Army ethos – *"Individual priorities subsumed by the needs of the mission."*[107] This, the paper argues, emphasises teamwork and leadership. To implement this strategy, in October 1998 the US Army produced PAM 600-3 *"The Commissioned Officer Development and Career Management Book"*[108] Apart from articulating career management policy for each separate branch of the US Army, PAM 600-3 considers in some detail the overarching principles of *"Officer Leader Development"*. Through Leader Development (LD), the US Army plans to implement the OPMS XXI vision of more effective officers. The consequence of OPMS XXI and Leader Development on young officers is illustrated in Figure 5 which charts the initial career development of a newly commissioned officer in the US Signal Corps:[109]

FIGURE 5
INITIAL CAREER DEVELOPMENT OF US ARMY YOS

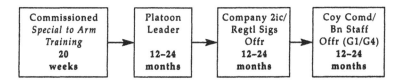

| Commissioned *Special to Arm Training* 20 weeks | Platoon Leader 12–24 months | Company 2ic/ Regtl Sigs Offr 12–24 months | Coy Comd/ Bn Staff Offr (G1/G4) 12–24 months |

Source: Colonel Charles R. Scott, PERSCOM,1999.

In essence, the impact of OPMS XXI at the formative stage of a YOs career is minimal as it primarily seeks to influence the career development of officers once they have been selected for promotion to Major. All officers should, ideally, experience a common grounding up to this point. On analysis it is apparent that the early stages of a US Army officer's career is very similar to his or her British counterpart; a succession of short appointments in order to gain experience and exposure to different levels of command. In the US Army these early appointments are sought after as they have to be successfully completed in order for an officer to be deemed *"Branch Qualified"* which is a pre-requisite for promotion to Major.

Bespoke HRM?

Interestingly, PAM 600-3 identifies that the US Army Officer Corps reflects American society as a whole and may span over four decades of age groups. Therefore career expectations, job satisfaction, discipline, priorities, leader abilities, educational aptitude, importance of family and cultural values vary widely among serving year groups. It is claimed that OPMS responds to the *"individual needs of the officer as well as the mission and requirements of the force."*[110]

During my interview with Colonel Scott he stated that there is an ongoing cultural change at PERSCOM following OPMS XXI. Career Managers are now making much more of a conscious effort to be more receptive to the career aspirations of the individual. Consequently they are working harder in order to provide a much more *"tailored"* service, or at least agree an acceptable compromise if there is a clash with the interests of the Army.

Assessing the Effectiveness of OPMS XXI

OPMS XXI effectively articulates where the US Army would like to go with its HRM programme. The vision of more effective leaders, developed through tactical assignments, formal education and self-development will enable both soldiers and units to be managed and organised more efficiently. In this respect OPMS XXI provides a firm foundation for change. In reality there has been, above all others, one fundamental policy change in the US Army officer career management system, which it is hoped will result in more tactical experience for *selected* officers. This is within the field of *"Functional Area"* employment.

Functional Area Employment

Apart from the *"Years of Service"* career management structure, the other key difference between the US and British Army is the employment of officers in secondary *"Functional Areas"*. Early on in an officer's career, at around the five-year point,[111] he or she decides (following negotiation and guidance from career managers) on a secondary area of military employment in addition to his or her's dedicated primary specialisation. These additional skills are designated *"Functional Areas"*[112] and create shadow employment for an officer when he or she is not in a primary post appointment. An example of *"Functional Area"* employment within the US Army is Human Resource Management. An officer within this discipline would divide his or her career between HRM-related appointments and his or her primary function (signals, armour, infantry etc). OPMS XXI has developed four overarching *"Career Fields"* which have collated and grouped together the previously independent *"Functional Areas"* (FA); these are

- **Operations** – approximately **66%** of officers will be employed within this *"Career Field"*[113]
  FA include; Psychological Operations and Civil Affairs.

- **Information Operations** – **9%** of officers.
  FA include; Information Systems Engineering, Strategic Intelligence & Simulations Operations.

- **Institutional Support** – **10%** of officers.
  FA include; HRM, Operations Research & Strategy and Force Development.

- **Operational Support** – **15%** of officers.
  FA include; Acquisition, Industrial Management and Systems Automation Engineering.

In developing *"Career Fields"*[114] OPMS XXI has directed that officers can now compete for promotion within their dedicated *"Functional Area"* as opposed to their primary employment area. Therefore under OPMS XXI, an HRM specialist would be considered for promotion only against all other HRM specialists from the *"Institutional Support Career Field"*. Allowing "specialists" to form their own career paths is recognition by OPMS XXI that the US Army has a need for non-operational *"Warfighters"* to fill certain requirements.[115] The fundamental change is that dependent upon which

"Career Field" an officer is assigned to determines the amount of time that he or she will spend in a tactical unit.

Under OPMS XX1, the only *"Career Field"* that demands significant service in tactical units is *"Operations."* Therefore, because the officers in the three remaining *"Career Fields"* are not required to embrace the *"Muddy Boots"* culture in order to get promoted, there are now enough tactical assignments available to fully develop those officers who have specialised in *"Operations."* One US Army Officer[116] described this new development as:

> *"OPMS XXI says that if you're a "Bill Gates" rather than a "Patton" or a "Slim" you should have the opportunity for advancement since technology is creating such a complex battlefield."*

Summary of US Army Career Management

Notwithstanding the many similarities between the US and British Army, in terms of ethos and *modus operandi* there are some fundamental differences within the career management area. The *"Years of Service"* structure is advantageous in that it allows all officers to compete on a "level playing field" and appears to work successfully in an army where there is a higher degree of acceptance with the career management system than in Britain. Whether Britain would embrace the concept of older officers in rank is debatable, but certainly the option of providing early responsibility that is not promotion-based is an initiative worthy of further consideration.

The concept of OPMS XXI is sound as it seeks to ensure that selected officers are exposed to as much tactical service as possible so as to prepare them for higher command. The strategic and holistic nature of officer HRM is identified, namely the impact of policies on;

- Officer Development
- Soldier management and leadership
- Unit efficiency

While OPMS XXI aspires to have a positive effect at more senior ranks within the US Army (Major and above) it is arguably making little difference to the career management and development of YOs. If anything US Army YOs are rotated through Platoon and Company command on a more frequent basis than their British counterparts; primarily because of the necessity to *"Branch Qualify"* all officers in platoon and company command prior to promotion to Major. This scenario is applicable to all officers, regardless of which *"Career Field"* they aspire to later join.

In a shrinking army the US has created a tiered effect that demands, following a common *"grounding"*, different levels of leadership and tactical ability from its officers dependent upon which *"Career Field"* they are employed in. In my view this would be an unworkable system for the British Army. This is primarily because the US system appears to stream officers' too early in their careers, thereby limiting flexibility and employability (important in a small army), while arguably creating an adversarial relationship[117] between the *"Operations"* elite (the group from which all command appointments are primarily selected)[118] and the other *"Career Fields"*.

However, in the US the creation of *"Career Fields"* has ensured that those officers who require prolonged exposure to tactical assignments are able to get it, which can only have a positive effect on those soldiers and units affected.[119] Although *"Career Fields"* do not begin to impact on an officer's career until the five year point there are obvious implications for career managers during the early stages of YOs careers as individuals are identified and "groomed" for their future specialisation. The inference here is that once an officer has been assigned a *"Functional Area"* at the five year point which is not within the Operations *"Career Field"*; it could subsequently impact on the type and quality of assignments between the five and ten year point. It is acknowledged, however, that an officer is given the opportunity at the 10 year point to apply to change his or her *"Functional Area"* in order to move to a better suited *"Career Field"*.

CONCLUSIONS

The aim of this chapter has been to analyse the effects of Royal Signals Young Officer career management policy. My research was primarily based on Peter Senge's work that considered the unintended negative 2nd and 3rd order effects of a fundamentally flawed single policy. The chapter argued that flawed YO *"Career Compression"* management policy impacted and influenced soldier career management and retention and also unit efficiency.

1st Order Effect – The YO

Rather than have the *"burden of proof"* to demonstrate that current YO career management policy is flawed (there are now sufficient official papers currently in circulation that have conclusively established this issue), the focus of this element of the chapter was therefore primarily on the *effects* of the policy on YOs. Following analysis of the survey and discussions with senior Royal Signals officers, I detected that amongst the current generation of YOs is a culture that is more orientated towards *"self"* rather than *"service"*. This culture has been conditioned by a career management system that is arguably too focused on continual movement and progression. A direct consequence of the policy is that YOs do not get an adequate period of time to gain valuable command and leadership experience, which as a result could restrict their effectiveness in more senior appointments.

2nd Order Effect – Soldier Career Management

Data was presented from Major Kelly's work, which indicated that Royal Signals soldiers are dissatisfied with a raft of career management related issues that are directly attributable to transient leadership at the troop level. Additionally, the survey carried out for this chapter identified that YOs acknowledge that the present career management system is detrimental to the career management of soldiers. There is a linkage on this issue between *"temporary"* Troop Commanders, a lack of formal quality management training on the Troop Commanders Course and the sometimes *"adversarial"* relationship between units and MCM Div regarding *"ownership"* of soldiers' careers. With this in mind, several initiatives were discussed that could have a positive impact on the current scenario.

3rd Order Effect – Unit Efficiency

There is an intuitive relationship between YO career management policy and unit efficiency that it difficult to quantify, given the vagaries of the constituent elements of the Moral Component of Fighting Power. There are numerous anecdotal examples that **imply** a negative 3rd order effect. Given that motivation, morale, leadership and management are a command function at **any** level; there **must** therefore be an indirect effect on unit efficiency as a result of current policy. Major Kelly's work and this chapter have both demonstrated majority views that indicate morale suffers through transient leadership which impacts on motivation and retention. From a personal view I consider that unit efficiency does suffer as a direct result of current YO career management policy.

I consider there is currently a disconnect between Army and Royal Signals HR Strategies and current YO career management. While it is acknowledged that the Grove Review has greatly influenced current manning policy, there has been a continuation within Royal Signals of the practice of *"quantity"* as opposed to *"quality"* appointments for YOs, even in the light of increased career compression. Although Royal Signals Manning and Career Management Division now advocates a one two-year appointment for Troop Commanders, it remains the whim of Commanding Officers to either leave YOs in the same troop or (more usually according to the survey) move them around for the sake of experience. In this respect, considering its subsequent negative impact on YOs, soldiers' career management and overall unit efficiency, my view is that the development of YOs could be more effectively managed.

At the operational and strategic level, the Army has produced a string of HR reviews that have offered much but produce minimal impact at the tactical level. They have had no significant influence on career management (a major factor in retention) and provide little in the way of policy guidance for Manning and Career Management Division. In this respect Army HRM is ineffective and should strive to address more *"micro"* issues in its next iteration.

NOTES

1. Wass de Czege, H. (Colonel, US Army). "How to Change an Army". *Military Review*, January–February 1997.
2. Applegate, D. (former Colonel Force Development LW4). "Towards The Future Army". *Strategic & Combat Studies Institute*. Number 36, September 1998, p. 77.
3. Wheeler R. (Chief of the General Staff). "A Vision for the Army". Speech at Adjutant General's Annual Conference – Managing Retention. London, 24th March 1999.
4. D/DM(A)/60/01 dated 14 Dec 1998. The Standing Committee on Army Manpower Forecasts (SCAMF). *Interim Manpower Assessment Report 1998/99*.
5. Aitken RHT (Colonel Employment Policy (Army)). "Retain – Defining the Problem". Speech at Adjutant General's Annual Conference – Managing Retention". London. 24th March 1999.
6. Harley A. (Adjutant General). Introduction to Adjutant General's Annual Conference – Managing Retention. London. 24th March 1999.
7. Palmer, AMD (Director General Army Training & Recruiting). "Challenges for the Army Training & Recruitment Agency (ATRA)". Speech at Adjutant General's Annual Conference – Managing Retention. London. 24th March 1999.
8. "Army Fears Crisis as Officers Pull Out". *Sunday Times*. 24th January 1999.
9. Rudden, T. DASA. Letter to Author, D/AS(M)1/33/5/1 dated 26th January 1999.
10. Senge PM *The Fifth Discipline: The Art and Practice of the Learning Organization*. Random House, London, 1990.
11. "*Only Shell and BT recruit more graduates than the Army*". Palmer, AMD. "Challenges for the Army Training & Recruitment Agency (ATRA)". Speech at Adjutant General's Annual Conference – Managing Retention. London. 24th March 1999.
12. Dryburgh J. (former SO2 Officers R Signals), "The Junior Officer's 'Truncated Career' ", *The Wire*. Vol.51 No.5, p. 41.
13. This was a key recommendation of the *Grove Review of Army Officer & Soldier Career Structures*, Final Report, p. 8. 4. March 1993.
14. Fitzalan Howard TM OBE (former Colonel, Military Secretary), *Presentation to British Army Staff Conference (BASCON), Washington DC*. 12th October 1997.
15. Robson, P. (Major, MS5). Military Secretary Presentation to RMCS. 9th December 1998.
16. Dryburgh, J. Op. cit, p. 42.
17. Wood N F Brigadier, [soinc@mail.army.mod.uk], "Officer Training", private e-mail to author [complin@cfcsc.dnd.ca], 28th January 1998.
18. This policy is likely to be compounded by the proposal of Director Manning (Army) to increase the entrance age to Sandhurst to 29 from 1st April 2000. Director Manning (Army) brief to author: *Career Structure 2000*. Marshall N (SO2 Officer Policy), DM(A), 24th March 1999.
19. *Royal Signals Prospectus*. Method Publishing , Sutherland, Scotland, 1995, p. 36.
20. The current SO2 Officers Royal Signals stated during interview that the current manning policy is, where possible, to ensure that YOs complete one 2 year tour in the same unit. Interview with Major SP Wallis MBE Royal Signals, RMAS, 6th May 1999.
21. HQ Land Command. *Retention of Soldiers in Land Command*. Attachment to HQ 3 (UK) Div. *Human Resources Planning – Retention*. HQ 3 (UK) Div G1/1405 dated 28th January 1999.

22. This statement was originally made by Brigadier JH Griffin (then Commander CIS, HQ Land Command), in a private e-mail to the author: [jgriffin@mail.army.mod.uk], "Officer Training", private e-mail message to Major GJ Complin [complin@cfcsc.dnd.ca], 10th December 1997. It was reiterated during an interview at HQ R Signals, Blandford Camp. 13th May 1999.

23. Senge PM. *The Fifth Discipline.* Op. cit., pp. 17–26.

24. Applewood – Catalyst for Discovery. *The Fifth Discipline: The Art and Practice of the Learning Organisation.* http://www.the-wire.com/applewood/senge. html.

25. Mission Command is a style of command adopted by the British Army that promotes "Decentralised command, freedom and initiative." See: *Army Doctrine Publication Volume 2 – Command.* HQDT/18/34/51 dated April 1995, pp. 2–4.

26. Ibid.

27. Bell W. *The Impact of Policies on Organisational Values and Culture.* http://www.usafa.af.mil/jscope/JSCOPE99/Bell99.html.

28. Bell W. "A Systems Dynamics Approach to the Decline of Trust and Risk Taking in the American Army". Brief to US Joints Chief of Staff Committee, 25th March 1999.

29. Ibid.

30. *Agenda for Officer Recruitment Working Group (ORWG) 2nd Meeting.* 4th March 1999. D/DM(A)/54/20 dated 26th February 1999, p. B-17.

31. A rise from 3.3% to 5.25% over 3 years. Source: *The Timing of Officer Career Courses.* D/AG/11100/7/28 DITrg Pol (A) dated 14th May 1999.

32. *Army Continuous Attitude Survey Report.* DERA/CHS/MID/CR990019/1.0 dated February 1999, p. 75.

33. Oppenheim AN. *Questionnaire Design, Interviewing and Attitude Measurement.* Pinter, London, 1996.

34. Yardley M. *Sandhurst: A Documentary.* Harrap, London, 1988, p. 108.

35. 'The academy where kings work to rule', *The Times.* 13th February 1999.

36. Interview with Brigadier SG Hughes CBE, Commander 2 (National Communications) Signal Brigade. Corsham, 24th May 1999.

37. A common theme from regiments was the negative effect of current operations on retention. For example 21 Signal Regiment (Air Support) is currently 70% committed to operations and can only offer its soldiers a 4-month respite between tours. Troop Commanders are therefore faced with a significantly more challenging task, given their short time in command, to create cohesion and maintain morale.

38. CO 21 Signal Regiment (AS) forcefully made this point. Interview with Lieutenant Colonel JA Terrington Royal Signals, Commanding Officer 21 Signal Regiment (Air Support) Colerne, 25th May 1999. Brigadier Cook also echoed this view. Interview with Brigadier JRB Cook, Commander 11 Signal Brigade. Shrivenham, 28th May 1999.

39. Interview with Brigadier JH Griffin, Signal Officer in Chief (Army). Blandford, 13th May 1999.

40. This term was coined in the post-Vietnam military in the US. It implies a culture whose leaders are "*too concerned about themselves to help subordinates sufficiently.*" The term "*Career Fear*" is now more commonly used to describe this phenomenon. See: Kellog D. *Career Fear: A Worm in the Core of American Military Values.* http://www.usafa.af.mil/jscope.JSCOPE99/Kellogg99.html.

41. Interview with Lieutenant Colonel ND Couch Royal Signals, Commanding Officer 3 (United Kingdom) Division Headquarters and Signal Regiment. Bulford, 25th May 1999.

42. Interview with Lieutenant Colonel M Lithgow MBE Royal Signals,

Commanding Officer 30 Signal Regiment. Bramcote, 3rd June 1999.
43. Interview with Lieutenant Colonel JA Terrington Royal Signals, Commanding Officer 21 Signal Regiment (Air Support).
44. Interview with Lieutenant Colonel ND Couch Royal Signals.
45. Interview with Brigadier JRB Cook, Commander 11th Signal Brigade. Shrivenham, 28th May 1999.
46. This is the point that was made when the work of Peter Senge was considered earlier; "I Am My Position". While people understand their daily tasks, they do not understand the purpose of the enterprises they take part in.
47. Officer Personnel Management System XXI Task Force Study – July 1997.
48. Interview with Brigadier SG Hughes CBE, Commander 2 (National Communications) Signal Brigade.
49. Beevor A. *Inside The British Army*. Chatto & Windus, London. 1990, p. 92.
50. Study Days are organised by units as a vehicle for Continuous Professional Development. They tend to expose personnel to various aspects of their profession not normally encountered.
51. Interview with Lieutenant Colonel JA Terrington Royal Signals, Commanding Officer 21 Signal Regiment (Air Support).
52. Interview with Lieutenant Colonel ND Couch Royal Signals, Commanding Officer 3 (United Kingdom) Division Headquarters and Signal Regiment. *Op Cit.*
53. This point was acknowledged and endorsed by Brigadier Griffin. Interview with Brigadier J. H. Griffin, Signal Officer in Chief (Army).
54. Segal D. and Sinaiko H. *Life in the Rank and File*. Pergamon-Brassey's, London. 1986, pp. 260–2.
55. Beevor A. *Inside The British Army*, p. 93.
56. Ibid. p. 89.
57. Bett M. *Independent Review of the Armed Forces' Manpower, Career and Remuneration Structures*. HMSO. 1995, p. 6.
58. Interview with Lieutenant Colonel ND Couch Royal Signals, Commanding Officer 3 (United Kingdom) Division Headquarters and Signal Regiment.
59. Lieutenant Colonel Lithgow was making specific reference to the lack of management training required to equip YOs to take a more proactive role in soldier career management. Additionally, he voiced concern at the lack of "*technical*" responsibility devolved to YOs, which in his view is required to ensure that mainstream Royal Signals officers and not "*Specialists*" remain the focal point for all aspects of Royal Signals operational planning and command. Interview with Lieutenant Colonel M. Lithgow MBE Royal Signals, Commanding Officer 30 Signal Regiment.
60. Baynes J. *The Soldier in Modern Society*. Eyre Methuen, London. 1972, p. 94.
61. Beevor A. *Inside The British Army*, p. 92.
62. Mileham P. "Ethos: British Army Officership 1962–1992". *Strategic & Combat Studies Institute*. Number 19, 1996, p. 46.
63. Army Briefing Notes, *The Army for Today*. DPR (Army), 1995, p. B4.
64. Kelly PM. *Why are Soldiers Leaving the Royal Signals Prematurely?* Number 10 Master of Defence Administration Course, Royal Military College of Science. December 1996.
65. Herzberg F. *The Motivation to Work*. Wiley, New York, 1959.
66. Headquarters Royal Signals. *Management Education and Training for Young Officers, Warrant Officers and Senior NCOs in R SIGNALS*. SOinC(A)/10/13 dated 20th July 1997.
67. Letter from Brigadier JH Griffin to all members of the Corps – Major and above. DO/SOinC(A) dated 3rd August 1998.
68. *Royal Signals Troop Commanders Course*. Issue 1, dated 10th March 1998.

69. The duration of the Troop Commanders course has been progressively compressed. At its peak prior to the Second World War it lasted 18 months, but again its content was primarily technical. Nalder R. *The History of British Army Signals in the Second World War.* Royal Signals Institution, London, 1953, p. 331.

70. Interview with Lieutenant Colonel M. Lithgow MBE Royal Signals, Commanding Officer 30 Signal Regiment. Bramcote, 3rd June 1999.

71. Examples included the writing of reports on personnel and counselling for soldiers on career and welfare matters. Royal Signals Training Development Team. *Job Analysis of the Royal Signals Troop Commander.* September 1996, p 5.

72. Ibid. Enclosure 1, p. 5.

73. DI Trg Pol (A). *Career Development into the 21st Century – A Scoping Paper.* D/AG/11300/4/9 DI Trg Pol (A). Dated 17th January 1997.

74. Headquarters Royal Signals. *Management Education and Training for Young Officers, Warrant Officers and Senior NCOs in R Signals,* p. 11.

75. The components of *"Fighting Power"* are, Conceptual = Doctrine, Moral = The Man, and Physical = The Hardware. Ibid.

76. Interview with Brigadier JH Griffin, Signal Officer in Chief (Army). Blandford, 13th May 1999.

77. *The Army Continuous Attitude Survey.* DERA/CHS/MID/CR990019/1.0 dated February 1999, p. 47.

78. Interview with Major SP Wallis MBE Royal Signals. SO2 Officers Royal Signals Manning and Career Management Division. Royal Military Academy Sandhurst, 6th May 1999.

79. Interview with Lieutenant Colonel T. W. Canham Royal Signals, Commanding Officer 11 Signal Regiment. Blandford, 2nd June 1999.

80. Interview with Lt Col J Terrington Royal Signals, Commanding Officer 21 Signal Regiment (Air Support). Colerne. 25th May 1999.

81. Brigadier Hughes endorsed this concept and suggested that it should form part of the next iteration of the Royal Signals HR Strategy. Interview with Brigadier SG Hughes CBE, Commander 2 (National Communications) Signal Brigade. Corsham, 24th May 1999.

82. Interview with Brigadier JRB Cook, Commander 11 Signal Brigade. Shrivenham, 28th May 1999.

83. *Staff Officers Handbook.* Army Code No 71038 DGD&D/18/35/54. 1996, pp. 8–30.

84. *Design for Military Operations – The British Military Doctrine.* Army Code No 71451 D/CGS/50/8. 1996, pp. 4–5.

85. Ibid. pp. 4-5 to 4-6.

86. A view endorsed by all senior officers interviewed.

87. Interview with Brigadier JRB Cook.

88. Interview with Brigadier SG Hughes CBE.

89. Interview with Lt Col JA Terrington Royal Signals.

90. It should be noted that that current US Army HR and Career Management Policy papers are *only* available via the Internet; hard copies are not produced.

91. Interview with Colonel Charles R. Scott.

92. Interview with Major SJ Whitmarsh, former US Special Forces Career Manager. Fort Bragg, 18th May 1999

93. Interview with Colonel Charles R. Scott.

94. In practice, promotion to Captain generally occurs after 3.5 years of service. Interview with Colonel Charles R. Scott. Signals Branch Chief, US Personnel Command Washington DC, 17th May 1999.

95. *The Army Continuous Attitude Survey.* Main Data Report. DERA/CHS/MID/CR990019/1.0, p. 65.

96. Interview with Colonel Charles R. Scott.
97. It is possible to command a company in the US Army as a Captain with as little as 4 years commissioned service. Additionally only 1 year is required in post to "qualify' in command. Interview with Colonel Charles R. Scott.
98. Kennedy JF Inaugural Address, 20th January 1961.
99. Focus Group held at Fort Bragg, North Carolina, 18th May 1999.
100. In US Army Parlance *"Tactical Assignments"* mean postings that are not headquarters or staff related, and do not necessarily entail the direct command of soldiers. For example, Adjutant, Operations Officer, and Squadron 2ic all fall into this category.
101. Approximately 5% of any *"Year Group"* will promote 1 year ahead of their peers.
102. Faires JE *An Officer Corps for the 21st Century*. OPMS XXI Brief. http://www2.army.mil/opms.Briefing.htm.
103. McChrystal S., Gardner J. and McHale T. *Bridging the Competence Gap: Developing Tactical Leaders for the Army of 2015*. US Army War College, Carlisle Barracks, PA, 1997, pp. 35–6.
104. Ibid. p. 37.
105. Rosenburger JD "Coaching the Art of Battle Command". *Military Review*. Vol LXXVI, May/June 1996, p. 27.
106. Officer Personnel Management System XXI Study, July 1997, pp. 4–5. http://www.army.mil/opms.
107. OPMS XXI – *Executive Summary*. http://www.army.mil/opms.Ex-sum.htm.
108. PAM 600-3. *The Commissioned Officer Development and Career Management Guide*. http://books.hoffman.army.mil/cgi-bin/boomgr/BOOKS.P600 3.
109. As a comparison, there are approximately 30,000 soldiers and 10,000 officers in the US Signal Corps compared to 8,200 and 900 respectively in the Royal Signals, representing 9% of the British Army. http://www.army.mod.uk/army.organise/index.htm.
110. Faires JE *An Officer Corps for the 21st Century*. OPMS XXI Brief.
111. Ibid.
112. There are a total of 18 *"Functional Areas"* of secondary employment. Interview with Colonel Charles R. Scott.
113. OPMS XXI – *Executive Summary*.
114. It is estimated that it will take approximately five years (2002 is the stated goal) to switch the entire US Army Officer Corps over to *"Career Fields"*
115. OPMS XXI – *Executive Summary*.
116. Interview with Major S J Whitmarsh.
117. Both Colonel Scott and Major Whitmarsh acknowledged this point.
118. Faires JE op. cit.
119. The concept is officially described as *"Preserving warfighting capability and increasing opportunities within speciality fields"*. OPMS XXI – *Executive Summary*.

4

'Train for Certainty – Educate for Uncertainty': Personal Development in the British Army

RICHARD BARTLE
Cranfield University, Royal Military College of Science

INTRODUCTION

In 1998 the new Labour government announced its Strategic Defence Review.[1] In Chapter Six "A Policy for People"[2] it laid out its plans to "enhance the attractiveness of a Service career". This involved increasing the emphasis on vocational training and education by the use of new schemes that would be closely linked to the Department for Education and Employment's "Learning Age" proposals. Supporting Essay Nine – "A Policy for People" fleshed out the proposals admitting that the main thrust behind the new emphasis on training and education was to improve recruiting and retention. The "Learning Forces" initiative, as it is called, would aim to provide "better opportunities for personal development linked to academic, vocational and professional qualifications".[3] Substantial sums of money would be provided to fund this initiative which would be "based upon the following principles:

- competence in key skills, related to national targets and rank/employment;
- the opportunity to gain recognised and transferable qualifications;
- funding for learning activities during and after service;
- provision of Personal Development Records;
- access to information, advice and modern learning facilities, irrespective of rank, age, employment or location;
- return the individual to the civilian workplace with added value".[4]

The 1999 Defence White Paper[5] endorsed the principles of the "Learning Forces" initiative as laid out in the SDR and expanded upon them. The main thrust of the scheme would be the Personal Development Record to be issued to every serviceman and woman. This would enable each participant to "plan, track and demonstrate their personal development".[6] This development would range from the basic skills of numeracy and literacy to degree courses. Partial funding for academic/vocational courses would be made available both during service and up to 10 years afterwards. Though much of this initiative is not new to the Armed Forces, the re-emphasis of the need for personal development as well as training is a recognition that today's employers and their employees can benefit greatly from development education.

BACKGROUND

To many the concept of training conjures up those tenets of Taylorism that required the employee to become skilled in precise, scientifically-designed manoeuvres to make the manufacturing process as efficient as possible. Many of these kinds of activity required little in the way of intellectual input from the operative. He or she was merely required to perform certain physical activities in a precise manner in a well-defined order. Though this may be still true in some industries today, for many the requirements of the knowledge-based world have necessitated a new approach that involves not only training but also the development of the employee. Training has for a long time been associated with development though there is much confusion about its precise meaning. For some it seems to have been little more than a device to differentiate 'modern' training from the over-prescribed training of the Taylor school. More recent approaches have broadened the interpretation of development to include a much wider range of activities than were previously considered.

Investors in People claim to be the only 'people quality standard'. They place great emphasis on training and development and stress that competitive advantage can be gained by investing in the people in an organisation. They make very little distinction between training and development. For them training *and* development is any activity that "develops skills, and/or knowledge, and/or attitude and/or behaviour".[7] Whilst development alone, according to them, is a term that is usually used in conjunction with training "to describe learning activities that enable people to realise their potential".[8] Others are much more specific and make a fundamental distinction between training and development. Bernadin and Russell[9] for example define training as:

"any attempt to improve employee performance on a currently held job or one related to it. This usually means changes in specific knowledges, skills, attitudes or behaviors".

Whilst development is:

"learning opportunities designed to help employees grow. Such opportunities do not have to be limited to improving employee's performance on their current job".

These are quite distinct definitions. To these authors training is job specific whilst development is a means whereby an organisation can help its employees to become better individuals. In their view, development is designed to educate people so that they acquire new skills and abilities that can make them more useful as a member of both the organisation and society.

These definitions do not, however, appear to fit with the specific developmental concept of CPD or Continuous Professional Development. The Institute of Personnel and Development are in the forefront of the movement for continuous development. They describe CPD as 'constantly updating one's *professional* knowledge throughout one's working life'[10] (authors italics). According to this definition, CPD is very job specific development, one might even suggest that it is training except for the fact that, as its name implies, it is usually applied to the professions – medicine, architecture, law and so on. CPD was introduced by some of these professions to address the natural competence decay that occurs as time elapses after initial qualification. Perhaps it is merely a polite euphemism to describe what is in effect continuation training designed to up-date professionals as the body of knowledge increases within their profession.

It has been suggested,[11] though, that there are two sorts of CPD – learning that is essential for achieving business objectives and learning that is aimed at personal development. This has led Pierce[12] to develop a CPD model (Figure 1). In it he identifies four different approaches to professional development

a. *Stagnant.* This describes an organisation in which neither management nor employees are interested in training and development. Pierce suggests that such organisations would benefit greatly from a programme such as Investors in People.

b. *Selfish.* Although admitting that selfish is perhaps too harsh a word, Pierce uses it to describe the kind of development that is embarked upon by an employee without regard for the employer's needs. This is personal development and although some would argue that it could be of value in employee development programmes, Pierce argues that it highlights the difference between personal development and professional development.

FIGURE 1
A MODEL FOR CPD

Learning for business goals	Short-sighted	Sophisticated
	Stagnant	Selfish

Learning for personal development

Source: Pierce D. "Are you a model of sophisticated CPD?" People Management. 26 September 1996.

c. *Short-sighted*. According to Pierce there are organisations, as well as employees, that have a narrow perspective. These he calls short-sighted because they recognise the need for training but fail to consider how to motivate people to participate. Such employers are pleased when employees embark on CPD but see it as being the responsibility of their staff to do in their own time and at their own expense.

d. *Sophisticated*. In this category are those organisations that recognise that long-term job security is a thing of the past and that the motivation to learn can be individual. Nevertheless, they will seek to promote learning but at the same time negotiate with individuals to seek to share the benefits and costs of CPD fairly.

Pierce admits that finding the right balance is difficult but suggests that the role of professionals is to persuade their employees to move towards the sophisticated corner of the model.

Whilst this model is a useful start point from which to examine development, the criticism of personal development that it is selfish and does not contribute much to an organisation runs contrary to contemporary thinking. Indeed, many would argue[13] that in today's learning organisation it is personal development as much as CPD that contributes to the knowledge base of the organisation. Thomason,[14] for example, as long ago as 1988 saw development as preparing people to 'perform work beyond that which currently engages them', in addition, he says, it also prepares them to accept responsibilities greater than they presently have. More recently, the government[15] recognised that all will benefit from investment in personal development. They believe that learning can contribute to the "self-reliance, self-confidence, employability and adaptability of individuals and that this will be of benefit, not only to those individuals, but also to the economy and communities". Personal development, they imply, is not a selfish act but one 'which complements the training provided by employers'.

In their White Paper,[16] *Learning to Succeed*, the government sets out its vision for the future. It sees employers and employees as partners who will both play a part in personal development. Individuals should be encouraged to take an active role in their own personal development 'assisted by intensive advice and support'. They should be encouraged to seek out new opportunities to "improve their knowledge and skills and to make their own investment in personal success". Employers, on the other hand, will be encouraged to take "responsibility for improving the skills of their workforce". So, perhaps this is not that far away from Pierce's 'sophisticated' category except that it does seem to include those developmental activities that he would call 'selfish'. The idea of a partnership in which employer and employee sit down and plan for personal development certainly fits in well with the 'sophisticated' model but the government's plans go further in that they require the acceptance that *all* development can be beneficial to both the organisation and the individual. This could even extend to the kind of unconventional developmental activity described by Plath[17] such as voluntary participation in an amateur dramatic society that builds leadership potential. He maintains that 'in employee development, results count, not delivery means'.

The same ideas were central to Drucker's[18] thoughts on development when he said that it should have two purposes; the first being the "health, survival and growth of the enterprise"; and the other being the "health, growth and achievement of the individual both in his capacity as a member of the organisation and as a person". Furthermore:

> "Development ... focuses on the person. Its aim is to enable a man to develop his abilities and strengths to the fullest extent and to find individual achievement. The aim is excellence".[19]

These sentiments were endorsed by, of all people, Henry Ford. Much vilified for his selective application of Frederick Taylor's principles of "Scientific Management" he, nevertheless, established as early as 1914 a school for immigrant workers who spoke little or no English.[20] During his lifetime he opened 74 schools with 'an emphasis on transferring academic knowledge to skills needed in the workplace'.[21] To this day Ford have a reputation for encouraging personal development. They recognise that 'today's workplaces need people who are flexible and adaptable; who have an intuitive ability to solve problems and work in teams; who are independent, creative thinkers; and who can communicate effectively'.[22] To that end Ford (UK) with the co-operation of the trades unions set up their Employee Development and Assistance Programme (EDAP). The Ford EDAP scheme is such a good example of an organisation's commitment to employee development that it is worth examining in more detail. Indeed, EDAP set the standard for employee development to such an extent that until recently such initiatives were collectively known as 'EDAP schemes'. They are run in each Ford plant by an EDAP Committee made up of management and union representatives. The committee is responsible for local EDAP policies as well as approving applications and monitoring the work of the local education staff who run the programme.[23] In addition to offering advice and information, EDAP offers educational guidance, help with enrolment, help and support during the course and financial assistance. The range of courses covers everything from academic and technical courses to artistic and creative pursuits. Employees can attend as many courses within one year as they like as long as they are within the EDAP limit but they must be taken within the employees' own time. John Crew, Operations Manager at Dagenham, believes that EDAP is a way of institutionalising lifelong learning and that this gives the company a competitive advantage because 'people who are committed to lifelong learning know how to deal with change, know how to upgrade their skills'.[24] This is endorsed by Alan Tuckett, director of NIACE (the National Association for Adult Continuing Education). He is convinced that any learning has benefits for the organisation, 'a passion for learning something like golf skills spills over into a passion for learning to do things differently and better'.[25]

Ford is rightly proud of the EDAP scheme and dedicates 2.7% of their payroll to education and training.[26] This is a scheme that can be used as a model for other personal development schemes primarily because it has stood the test of time. However, it also deals with most of the "CPD dilemmas" described by Sandra Clyne[27] in her book *Continuing Professional Development*. Although aimed specifically at CPD, her list of dilemmas offers a spectrum of methods for managing educational development and raises fundamental questions about the relationship between employee and employer in a personal development scheme. The Ford EDAP scheme falls firmly on the side of free choice for the employee in that it:

- does not have a prescriptive structure
- puts the onus on the individual to decide whether or not to become involved
- focuses on the learning outcomes of the development process
- supports learners both financially and with advice
- does not monitor the progress of learners but trusts them to do it
- legitimises personal development
- stresses the benefits of personal development
- does not penalise those who do not participate
- is based upon wide consultation with membership

In this scheme, therefore, it can be said that the employees are in charge of their own development but it is there for the benefit of the employer as well as the learner.

Though much of the past work on development has stressed its link with training, recently there has been a growing emphasis on the advantages of learning itself. Schemes such as the Ford Employee Development and Assistance Programme have encompassed all learning experiences be they academic or technical courses, artistic or creative pursuits. The rationale behind these approaches is that all forms of learning have a beneficial outcome for both partners in the contract. The employee becomes more flexible and adaptable; develops an intuitive ability to solve problems and work in teams; becomes an independent creative thinker; and can communicate more effectively.[28] The employer attracts and retains the best employees and develops them into people who are trained to learn so that they have a better chance of dealing with the change that is bound to occur during the course of their careers. The Army has developed its own scheme in much the same way as Ford and sees its advantages as being primarily in recruiting and retention but they also stress the promotion of a flexible workforce and the maximisation of individual potential.[29]

ARMY LEARNING FORCES AND PERSONAL DEVELOPMENT

Learning and personal development in the Army can trace its origins back at least to 1772 when a Military Society for the scientific study of Gunnery was set up at Woolwich.[30] Gradually this developed first, into the Royal Artillery Institute and then the Artillery College. The introduction of the Advanced Course for Artillery Officers in 1864 is widely recognised as the official beginning of the Royal Military College of Science. Indeed, due to the great emphasis placed upon mathematics, the first Professor of Mathematics, the Reverend Francis Bashforth was then appointed.

Soldiers' education came later. It began in the regimental schools that emerged at the beginning of the 19th century.[31] By 1857 compulsory education for all recruits was introduced, only to be abolished thirty years later. "It was not until 1913 ... that recruits were again compelled to attend school during the first six months of their service".[32] By this time a system of certificates ranging from 1st to 4th Class, and connected to promotion, had been introduced. In one form or another this remained in place until the early 1970s when soldier education was reformed. Running in parallel with this formal educational development system was another less formal, non-prescriptive scheme introduced during World War I. This originally consisted of informative lectures given by visiting academics on "such information on the current topics as could be accurately gathered and safely given".[33] This was soon extended to cover subjects that would help soldiers to resettle in civilian life at the end of the war. Courses were open to all ranks and within two months of their inception 6000 troops had enrolled and there were another 6000 waiting for classes to be opened.[34] Thus began a bipartite system of development that survives to this day in which education, on the one hand, is formally tied to promotion and, on the other, is available for personal development.

Educational Development

For officers the formal part of their educational development begins at the Royal Military Academy Sandhurst (RMAS or just Sandhurst) where they embark upon a forty-two week course of both military and academic instruction. This attracts a half credit exemption for an Open University Degree and has recently been accredited by the Institute of Personnel and Development for the award of LicIPD. After Sandhurst education continues under the Junior Officers' Training and Education Scheme where emphasis is placed upon the development of written skills with a series of research papers. Following a period of regimental service the Integrated Promotion and Staff Examination selects officers both for promotion to Major and selection for further Staff training. Various courses are open to those selected for Staff training all of which lead to the award of a Master's degree from Cranfield University. For most officers this ends the formal part of their educational development though some are selected for the Higher Command and Staff Course and even fewer still attend the Royal College for Defence Studies. To all intents and purposes, though, the formal element of officers' educational development ends in their late thirties/early forties.

Soldiers also have a series of formal educational development courses that are tied to promotion. These are known as Education for Promotion (EFP) courses and are examined at two levels - EFP1 for promotion from Corporal to Sergeant and EFP 2 for promotion to Warrant Officer. The latest version of the EFP scheme was introduced in 1994 and at both levels consists of an integrated course based upon "job related military skills, knowledge and attitudes".[35] Subjects such as Communication Skills, Arithmetic, Management and Current Affairs are incorporated into two subject areas – Army and Defence Studies and Military Management Studies. Success on the course is determined by a system of rigorous on course assessment and testing.

As part of the "Learning Forces" initiative announced in the SDR, soldiers who successfully complete these courses are encouraged to gain nationally recognised qualifications such as NVQs/SNVQs and certificates in management and supervision. To that end arrangements are now in place for personnel attending EFP 1 courses to enrol on a Certificate and NVQ Level 3 in Supervisory Management whilst those studying at the higher EFP2 level can enter for a Certificate and NVQ Level 4 in Management. A satisfactory portfolio of evidence of certain management competences performed in the workplace has to be produced after the relevant EFP course before these qualifications can be awarded. Holders of EFP1 and EFP 2 qualifications can also apply for National Examining Board for Supervision and Management awards of the Introductory Certificate in Management and the Certificate in Management respectively. In this way the Army is working towards the achievement of the government's new National Learning Targets[36] of 50% of adults with NVQ level 3 and 28% of adults with NVQ level 4.

The White Paper – "Post 16: Learning to Succeed" also sets a target of a 7% reduction in non-learners. The Army, like many employers, is acutely aware of the problems caused by approximately 23% of the adult population being unable to cope with the three 'R's. Figures are not available but inevitably the Army has its share of recruits with difficulties with basic skills. The problem for the Army is in targeting accurately those with such problems. At the present time, trials are being carried out by members of the Adjutant General's Education and Training Support Branch along with local colleges, the Basic Skills Agency and the British Dyslexia Association to see if it possible to distinguish dyslexia from basic skills problems.[37] Reports suggest that these trials have been successful though highly labour intensive. Future plans are initially to offer basic skills courses at nine Army Education Centres (AECs) followed subsequently by ETS officers playing a monitoring role in placing soldiers in appropriate civilian-run basic skills courses that are recommended by the Basic Skills Agency. Further work with the British Dyslexia Association is underway to produce identification procedures for dyslexics and to provide basic remediation packages.

Personal Development

Following on from the ad hoc arrangements for personal development that began during World War I, the Army has continued to encourage learning in the widest possible context for all ranks. Classes in AECs, correspondence courses, libraries, money and advice have been made available for all kinds of personal development ranging from Open University degrees to pottery classes and from language courses to household maintenance. The Army's rationale for this is similar to that for the Ford EDAP scheme – the development of the habit of lifelong learning. Like Ford, the Army believes that this will produce 'people who are flexible and adaptable; who have an intuitive ability to solve problems and work in teams; who are independent, creative thinkers; and who can communicate effectively'.[38]

The announcement of the Learning Forces initiative in the SDR has been followed by more details of the arrangements for personal development in all three services. Central to the new scheme is the introduction of a Personal Development Record (PDR) for all servicemen and women. Though new to the services PDRs have been in vogue for some time. The Army's scheme is based upon the recommendations of the Institute for Personnel and Development for a systematic approach to personal development. The IPD's key initial steps for recording and planning personal development[39] are:

- Undertaking an audit of current know how and competence.
- Setting aims and objectives in terms of future achievement both from a work-related and a personal development perspective.
- Identifying the knowledge and expertise necessary to achieve the aims and objectives set for development
- Making comparisons between existing knowledge and competences and the aims and objectives for development and identifying gaps that will form the basis of a development plan.

These steps are mirrored in the Army's PDR file that has been issued on a trial basis to the 4th Division.

Both a retrospective and a prospective approach is taken in the Army PDR file. Contained within a well-presented glossy file is contains a series of sections dealing with the recording of past achievements. Included within these are:

- Personal history – in which will be recorded personal details and non-military qualifications.
- Military history – for recording past training courses, promotions, achievements etc.
- Reports – this section is for the storage of annual and mid-year appraisal reports plus course reports and certificates (for which plastic files are provided).

A section is then provided for the assessment of these achievements so that the individual can identify his/her strengths and weaknesses in order to make decisions on future development and to prepare for interviews either with their reporting officer or educational advisers.

The prospective approach then deals with the "process of planning to learn, taking and making learning opportunities and reviewing ... the learning gained from [this] approach".[40] To that end there are sections both for military career planning and for personal planning. Due to the significant differences in special-to-arm requirements for military career planning, there will be special inserts for each cap badge giving career advice for each specific Arm or Service. This should enable servicemen and women to make the best decisions when they reach important crossroads in their military careers. The personal planning section, on the other hand, gives advice on the various routes available for personal development as well as suggestions on how to produce a Curriculum Vitae. Thus the PDR will take a soldier through the IPD recommended process of retrospectively examining past achievements and prospectively identifying possible areas for future personal development.

The Navy have already completed a pilot scheme for the Personal Development Record and plan to issue their version of the PDR to all new recruits from April 2000 and to all serving personnel later this year.[41] The Army and the RAF have pilot schemes under way.[42] The Army trial with 4 Division is due to be completed by June 2000 and the implementation to begin from September 2000. Though this trial is not completed at this time, early reports suggest that the PDR has proved popular across all ranks.[43]

Though a vital part of the Army's approach to personal development, the PDR is only one part of a comprehensive system for personal development that utilises a number of military and civilian agencies to provide the best possible advice and assistance to would-be students. In its new format it unifies a number of pre-existing but separate schemes that included language training, resettlement, the correspondence course scheme and various educational and recreational development courses. Resettlement remains separate from the Learning Forces Initiative though many courses embarked upon under the scheme will have resettlement benefits. All other developmental courses come under the Learning Forces Initiative which, though emphasising that Army personnel are ultimately responsible for their own personal development, offers a number of possible sources of advice for the would-be student both within the scheme and elsewhere. Within the scheme there are three military options beginning with the individual's reporting officer who will probably be only able to offer advice about development appertaining to the military career. This can be augmented with further advice from the Regimental Career Management Officer. But detailed advice on particular aspects of personal development is available from the ETS Personal Development Advisers who are based at local Army Education Centres. One hundred and five Personal Development Advisers are currently undergoing training with the College of Guidance Studies to improve their ability to give advice.[44] Their training will be finished by December 2000. The officers who complete this course will provide a professional advice service on personal development for all Army personnel. Additional advice will also be available from civilian sources including the new government help-line – Learning Direct - and local personal development providers such as FE Colleges, TECs and Learning Partnerships.

As well as offering advice, the new Army scheme provides financial assistance for many personal development courses. A new "Learning Credits Scheme" is being developed to encourage servicemen and women "to undertake academic or vocational education outside the work environment".[45] Two types of financial assistance are being made available. The first is known as Standard Learning Credits and it replaced the previous Individual Refund Scheme on 1 April 1999. Individuals taking advantage of this scheme can claim "80%

of fees up to a maximum of £175 annually for educational and vocational courses undertaken as part of personal development".[46] The precise scope of "educational and vocational courses" is currently being debated. Under the old Refund Scheme there were strict guidelines for the award of refunds for courses. Fundamentally they required the claimant, prior to a course, to demonstrate the benefits to the Army of attending that course – in other words Pierce's sophisticated approach.[47] For example a course in Cantonese Cookery could be considered to be beneficial to an army cook and so would be eligible for a refund under the old scheme. But the ordinary serviceman or woman would generally be ineligible for a refund of fees on the grounds that the service would not benefit from their attendance on such a course. In view of the government's expressed desire for "everyone to benefit from the opportunities that learning brings both in personal growth and the enrichment of communities"[48] a strong argument is being made for all courses to be eligible for learning credits under the new scheme. The outcome of this debate is eagerly awaited.

The second part of the scheme, known as Enhanced Learning Credits, is very similar to the government's Learning Accounts announced in the White Paper "Learning to Succeed".[49] In essence it is designed to provide individuals with substantial sums of money for Higher Education. Those participating will be required to invest £20 per month for up to six years. In return they will have access to a maximum of £6000 at specific points in their military career and for up to 10 years after leaving the Service. At the time of writing, the rules are still being drafted for this scheme but it is intended to implement it by Autumn 2000.

Though precise details of this second scheme are not available it is possible to comment on the monitoring arrangements for the first. Students are required to register before attending a course. This has to be agreed with a Personal Development Adviser. Initially, the student will be required to pay the full cost of the course upon enrolment. On completion of the course, the refund can then be claimed under the Standard Learning Credits scheme. So, the Army is able to monitor the student's attendance at and completion of a course. However, it is not clear from this system whether students completing examined courses have actually passed the course or not especially as disclosure and subsequent recording of a qualification is the responsibility of the individual. Obviously, this may pose a problem for the Army in monitoring the system fully. On the other hand, it may be that, in a similar way to the Ford EDAP scheme, the Army has chosen to have only a limited monitoring system and to trust students to complete their courses successfully.

CONCLUSIONS

The Army's response to the challenges set for employees by the government White Paper – "Learning to Succeed" – has been swift. It has reorganised existing schemes and devised new ones to produce a comprehensive system that positively encourages servicemen and women to develop the habit of lifelong learning. To that end it provides opportunities for personnel to gain recognised civilian qualifications such as NVQs/SNVQs, membership of professional bodies, first degrees and post graduate qualifications. At the heart of the new systems is a well thought out method for both a retrospective and a prospective approach to personal development based upon an individual's Personal Development Record. The sturdy, well-designed loose leafed binder in which soldiers will be encouraged to record past achievements and to plan for future development is both innovative and inspirational. It embraces the principles set out by the IPD for personal development records and, if used properly, cannot fail to be a significant aid to those wishing to undertake further education. Allied to this record is the comprehensive structure for assistance and advice based primarily around service facilities, in particular the soon-to-be trained ETS Personal Development Advisers. Their expertise should ensure that servicemen and women are given the best advice and encouragement with the added advantage of it being tempered by an understanding of the problems of learning in a service environment that only serving officers can provide. Financial assistance through Standard Learning Credits, whilst not as generous as the Ford EDAP scheme, is still significant. It could be even better if recognition is given to the benefits for the Army from ALL types of personal development and thus, like Ford, the Army offers financial assistance for any developmental course. Enhanced Learning Credits will also provide a strong incentive for personnel to embark upon higher education and the extension of the scheme to ten years after leaving the service must provide encouragement to those considering investing in the scheme. The new Army schemes for personal development have been introduced for a number of reasons, primarily, to improve recruitment and retention – a pressing need at this time. Like many good employers the Army recognises that personal development can both attract new recruits and retain existing personnel. It wishes to be seen as a "long term career of first choice".[50] It now recognises that there are "major benefits to be gained from encouraging and assisting [personnel] to invest in lifelong learning to improve personal knowledge and skills, to enhance career prospects and to increase future civilian employability".[51] The "Learning Forces" initiative is an imaginative scheme that will stand comparison with the best (including the Ford EDAP scheme). Whether it has an impact on recruitment and retention, only time will tell. What is clear is that once this scheme begins to work the Army cannot fail to benefit from encouraging, through personal development, the habit of lifelong learning in its workforce. However, the enterprise has only just begun. Without continued support even the best schemes can founder. In order to gain maximum benefit from the Learning Forces Initiative the Army, through its ETS Personal Development Advisers, must continue to encourage its workforce to make full use of their PDRs. In so doing, service men and women can take control of their own personal development and thus ensure that this innovative scheme reaches fruition.

NOTES

1. Ministry of Defence. *Strategic Defence Review: Modern Forces for a Modern World*. 1998. http://www.mod.uk/policy./sdr.htm.
2. Ibid. http://www.mod.uk/policy.sdr.chapt06.htm. p. 1 of 5.
3. Ibid. http://www.mod.uk/policy.sdr/essay09.htm. p. 4 of 19.
4. Ibid. p. 5 of 19.
5. Ministry of Defence. *Defence White Paper 1999*. http://www.mod.uk/policy.wp99.htm.
6. Ibid. http://www.mod.uk/policy.wp99.ch4.htm. p. 4 of 19.

7. *Investors in People Standard*. Investors in People (UK), 1998. See Glossary of Terms.
8. Ibid.
9. Bernadin H. J. and Russell J. E. A. *Human Resource Management – An Experiential Approach.* 2nd ed., Irwin/McGraw Hill, 1998, p. 172.
10. *Qualification Routes*. Institute of Personnel and Development, 1996.
11. Pierce D. "Are you a model of sophisticated CPD?" *People Management*. 26th September 1996, p. 59.
12. Ibid.
13. See for example: Anthony W. P. et al. *Strategic Human Resource Management.* 2nd Ed., The Dryden Press, 1996, p. 319: Armstrong M. *A Handbook of Personnel Management Practice*. 6th Ed., Kogan Page, 1996, p. 508: Bernadin H. J. & Russell J. E. A. Op. cit., p. 172.
14. Thomason G. A. *A Textbook of Human Resource Management*. IPM Publications, 1988, p. 298.
15. DfEE White Paper. *Post 16: Learning to Succeed.* , 1999, p. 3.
16. Ibid.
17. Plath A.R. "Training and Development". In Cornelius N. *et al..*, *Human Resource Management: A Managerial Perspective*. International Thompson Business Press, 1999, p. 72.
18. Drucker P.F., *Management: Tasks, Responsibilities and Practises*. Heinemann, 1974, p. 425.
19. Ibid. p. 426.
20. Pestillo P. J. "The War for Talent". *Vital Speeches of the Day*. New York, 15th October 1999, pp. 13–15.
21. Ibid.
22. Ibid.
23. Ingham R. "Ford's EDAP adds a Cybercafe". *Individual Learning.* Issue 6, November 1998. http://www.lifelonglearning.co.uk/iln6000/iln6001.htm
24. Ibid.
25. Ibid.
26. Ford Motor Company – Community Involvement. "Better Ideas: Corporate Citizenship". http://www.ford.com.default.asp?pageid=399&storyid=401.
27. Clyne S. "The Way Ahead". In idem, *Continuing Professional Development: Perspectives on CPD in Practice*. London, Kogan Page, 1995, p. 202.
28. Pestillo P. J. Op. Cit., p. 4.
29. D/AG/DETS(A)/1567-1 paper dated 11 January 2000. "Learning Forces and Personal Development: Summary of Army Progress as at December 1999".
30. See Anon. *A Celebration: Royal Military College of Science 50 Years at Shrivenham*. Royal Military College of Science, 1996.
31. White A. T. C. *The Story of Army Education 1643–1963*. London, Harrap, 1963.
32. Ibid. p. 41.
33. Lord Gorell quoted in Ibid. p. 47.
34. Ibid. p. 48.
35. Defence Council Instruction No 63. "Revised Education for Promotion Scheme". 1993.
36. DfEE White Paper. *Post 16: Learning to Succeed.* http://www.dfee.gov.uk/post16/br_white, 1999, Chap. 1, p.2.
37. D/AG/DETS(A)/1567-1 paper dated 11 January 2000. "Learning Forces and Personal Development: Summary of Army Progress as at December 1999".
38. Pestillo P. J. Op.cit.
39. Institute of Personnel and Development. *The IPD Policy and Guidelines on CPD*. Issued October 1997.
40. Bond C. "A Portfolio-based Approach to Professional Development". In Clyne S. *Continuing Professional Development: Perspectives on CPD in Practice*. London,

Kogan Page, 1995, p. 146.
41. D/DNSC/2710/11/9 dated 19 Oct. 1998. "The RN/RM Personal Development Record". Paras 6 and 7.
42. Ministry of Defence. *Defence White Paper 1999*. http://www.mod.uk/policy/wp99.htm.
43. D/AG/DETS(A)/1567-1 paper dated 11 January 2000. "Learning Forces and Personal Development: Summary of Army Progress as at December 1999".
44. Interview with Lt. Col. T. Moore AGC (ETS), 21 February 2000.
45. Land Command General Routine Order No. 134. *The Learning Forces Initiative*. December 1999.
46. Ibid.
47. Pierce D. Op. cit.
48. DfEE White Paper. Post 16: Learning to Succeed. , 1999, Chap. 1 p. 2.
49. Ibid.
50. Ritchie A. S. "Turning the Tide: Addressing Army Personnel Issues". *RUSI Journal*. Vol. 14, No. 6, Dec. 1999, p. 69.
51. Ibid.

5

Past, Present and Future: The Territorial Army Beyond SDR

RICHARD HOLMES
Cranfield University, Royal Military College of Science

This is neither a wholly academic paper nor a military memoir, but parts of both, for it reflects both the author's academic specialism, as a military historian with a particular interest in morale and motivation, and a Territorial who defied expectation (not least his own) by rising from private to brigadier in a career which has lasted more than thirty years. It must be emphasised from the outset that this neither necessarily reflects the opinion of the Ministry of Defence, where the author served at the time of writing, nor does it embody information which cannot be found in open sources. This is very much a personal view, and if, on the one hand, it may be illuminated by individual experience it must, on the other, be prey to that subjectivity which experience so often brings with it. Its focus is upon the TA, although much of what is said has relevance to the Volunteer Reserves of the other services.

We live in an age of military revolutions, real or putative. Many argue that a 'Revolution in Military Affairs' is already in the process of 'transforming the character of war by allowing the conduct of information warfare'.[1] The transformation in international politics signalled by the collapse of the Berlin Wall was scarcely less than revolutionary, and if change in western societies, encapsulating such things as the tendency for populations to become less deferential, more questioning, increasingly litigious and more devoted to 'Me PLC' has occurred gradually, its effect on armed forces has nonetheless been profound. The Territorial Army (TA) stands at the very epicentre of all these changes. It must cope with the impact of military technology; adjust to the new world, not hanker after the old; and (more closely integrated than Regular forces with the civilian society from which both spring) deal, promptly and effectively, with the impact of social change. At the time of writing it has begun to do all these things, and although it is not yet steering its new course with confidence, it is the author's contention that the way ahead is visible.

That this course is perilous there can be no doubt. On the one hand lies the rock of military conservatism, so attractive to many of those who grew up in a TA committed to the unfought war in NATO's central region. It would have been all or nothing; the political background to mobilisation, embodying a very serious crisis in which the national interest was evidently at stake, would scarcely have been contentious; the requirement for the Queen's Order to be signed meant that the mobilisation of reserves could not have been undertaken lightly; units would have gone to war together, and (despite the traditional tensions between Regular and non-Regular forces) there was, quite evidently, a job to be done for which too few Regulars were available. In 1988, for example, the TA provided 55,000 men in formed units to bring the British Army of the Rhine up to strength, reinforced the UK Mobile Force with another 5,000, and provided 27,000 men and women, the bulk of the forces for home defence, and it did so at an annual cost of about 5% of the army element of the Defence Vote.[2] Major General Murray Naylor, speaking to the RUSI in June 1992, observed that the fact that over 50% of the infantry assigned to the Germany-based 1 (British) Corps had been TA was 'perfectly logical and sustainable ...'.[3] The same year Colonel Christopher Day, a Regular officer then about to command a Territorial unit (the inimitable Royal Yeomanry) accurately described 'the material advantage to the nation of keeping the full-time army at the size that we *know* we need, maintaining the balance which we *might* need in a part-time state.'[4] However, writing as he was at a time when the old certainties had begun to fade, he went on to observe that it could not be, or purport to be, as ready as the regular army: it was 'an army in reserve, not a mobilised force.'[5] He sketched out a way ahead in which 'each individual TA unit is simultaneously a training depot, a holding unit for individuals who are readily available to the regular army, and a unit capable of mobilisation in its own right ... '.[6]

Colonel Day's balanced and prescient observations

pointed to what many Territorials regarded then (and some regard now) as the whirlpool, in which Territorials might be mobilised individually or in sub-units for operations which might fall well short of major war; which might see them serving in unfamiliar units; and which might snatch them from job and family at a time when mobilisation was, perhaps, not perceived as being a matter of national necessity. All the certainties of the old world (and how curiously *jolie laide* that world sometimes looks) have been swept away, and in the place of a TA facing a low risk of substantial mobilisation we have a TA facing a much greater chance of mobilisation on a smaller scale. To thrive in the next decade the TA must be steered between the rock and the whirlpool, remaining usable in and relevant to the new world, while at the same time not being used so frequently, or on such a scale, that it becomes unsafe for married men with serious jobs. Charting this course is the essence of this paper. Its structure is part chronological, part analytical, for the author believes that we can only understand the TA's future if we consider its history.

The TA formed in 1908 embodied three distinct strands. First was the militia, the old 'Constitutional Force', which could trace its origins to the Elizabethan militia and the Trained Bands of the Civil War. By 1900 the militia had become what Peter Dennis terms 'little more that a recruiting vehicle for the Regular Army, into whose ranks some 35 per cent of its members passed each year ...'.[7] The militia closely reflected the social structure of the Regular army of its day, with working-class NCOs and men officered by the more well-to-do, and the 'militia back-door' was a portal through which at least two future field-marshals – John French and Henry Wilson – entered Regular service. Next came the Yeomanry, initially formed from horse-owning 'gentlemen and Yeomanry' to combat the threat of French invasion in the Napoleonic period, officered and manned by those with socially conservative instincts, and likely to prove reliable when used, as Yeomanry units often were, in aid to the civil power in the rural and urban unrest of the 1820s and 1830s. Lastly, the Volunteers, like the Yeomanry, had been inspired by the threat of Napoleonic invasion: they saw a tremendous resurgence in the 1860s. There was less social distinction between officers and men than in the Regular Army or the militia: in one Middlesex Rifle Volunteer battalion all ranks wore swords when not on parade. As Stanley Simm Baldwin has written of the 1860s, 'those early Volunteers tended to be men who could afford to join their unit; like joining a club, you had to pay to belong to it. You had to pay your fare to the range and to camp and for your uniform and ammunition.'[8] Many units favoured uniforms of 'French grey', deliberately emphasising their social distinction from beery red-coated Regulars. Their members were often the butt of cartoonists, whose impish urchins asked bewhiskered tradesmen, thinly disguised as Volunteer officers, if they might 'wipe the blood off your sword, general?'[9]

Edward Cardwell's army reformed included 'territorialisation,' inaugurated in 1881, which formed county regiments from the old numbered regiments of the line: the 37th and 67th, for example, became 1st and 2nd Battalions of the Hampshire Regiment. Volunteer battalions gradually became numbered battalions of these regiments, although – like Princess Beatrice's Own Isle of Wight Rifles – they often retained old titles bracketed after their new battalion numbers.

The Territorial Force (TF), the TA's direct ancestor, came into being on 1 April 1908 during R. B. Haldane's restructuring of the army in the wake of its less than perfect performance in the Boer War. Haldane created County Associations – more recently Territorial and Auxiliary Forces Associations (TAVRAs) and, from April 2000, Reserve Forces and Cadet Associations (RFCAs) – to win over the 'natural leaders' in each county, and to run some of the force's functions, like recruiting and accommodation, at arm's length from the War Office. As part of Haldane's reform infantry militia units became Special Reserve battalions of infantry regiments (usually numbered 3rd, though there were some exceptions), which were, in effect, draft-finding units for Regular battalions, based on Regular depots, and were not expected to go to war as units. Yeomanry regiments and Territorial battalions (the latter often – though not universally, for this is, after all, the British Army – numbered 4th and 5th) were, however, expected to be mobilised and fight as units. However, they were not obliged to serve abroad, although their members might volunteer to do so – and received a natty

'Imperial Service' badge, worn on the right breast, to denote their availability for foreign service.

Thus, while Special Reserve and Territorial battalions seemed superficially similar, in that both were composed of voluntary part-timers, they were in practice very different. The former were essentially Regular soldiers in waiting, whose units lacked the strong sense of corporate identity and did not reflect the fierce localism arising from the fact that Territorial companies (and sometimes even detached platoons) had their own drill-halls. When young George Ashurst – 'fed up with being out of work and getting jobs and not being able to take them on' – tried to join the Regular army in 1913 the recruiting sergeant sensibly suggested that he should try the Special Reserve first. 'When you get in the army you might not like it, so I will tell you what to do', he said. 'Join the Special Reserve. which means that you will do six months in the barracks and seven years on the reserve, with just a month's camp each year.'[10]

Over the next ninety years the army's volunteer reserves underwent repeated change. In 1914 the presence at the War Office of Lord Kitchener – 'who had nothing but contempt for the entire concept of the Territorial Force'[11] – led to the sidelining of the TF and the County Associations in favour of the 'New Armies', raised directly through the Adjutant General's branch at the War Office. Despite this, 318 Territorial battalions served overseas, in comparison with 404 New Army battalions, and one historian has concluded that Kitchener's failure to recognise the 'mundane but essential nature' of the work done by County Associations had lasting disadvantages.[12] After distinguished service on all the war's fronts – many Regular officers found themselves echoing Brigadier-General C.B. Prowse, 'I did not think much of Territorials, but by God they can fight'[13] – the TF was reformed as the Territorial Army in 1920.

Some of the discussions surrounding the TA's formation in 1920 have a decidedly modern ring. Its members were now liable for foreign service, and although most County Associations recognised that without this the TA would have no future, some feared that there were insufficient guarantees that liability would only be applied in extreme circumstances, suspecting that the new TA might find itself providing drafts for that all too familiar creature, an over-deployed and under-recruited Regular army. There were, as Peter Dennis puts it, 'widespread fears that enlistment in the Territorial Force might jeopardise a man's employment', or that employers might not grant men leave to attend annual camp.[14] An attempt to impose a legal obligation on employers as a means of sharing the burden of national defence soon foundered, although there were repeated attempts to improve relations with employers at both the local and the national level.

The TA's ambiguous response to the civil unrest of the 1920s, when some of its members joined the officially-sponsored Civil Constabulary Reserve while others did not, underlined the danger of stretching the loyalty of those who live amongst the community they serve, but did not prove a long-term challenge to the force. It seems clear that the lessons of this episode have been well-learnt, for although the modern TA can be used in aid of the Civil *Community* – a process facilitated by Reserve Forces Act 1996 (RFA 96), and one which many Territorials would like to see used more often – it must not be used in aid to the Civil *Power*. Indeed, even after RFA 96 which, as we shall see, has made it easy for Territorials to slip into and out of full-time service without losing their status as reservists, those who wish to serve with Regular units in Northern Ireland, where the army has been deployed in aid of the Civil Power, must undergo a change of formal status, becoming Regular soldiers for the duration of their service there. Some of the TA's supporters look admiringly at the US National Guard, which, from its inception, has had a significant Civil Power emphasis. While there are some aspects of the Guard's organisation which merit our admiration (the TA's recruiting and retention might profit, for instance, from some of the financial incentives on offer to the Guard) the author's own experience as a member of a Chicago-area National Guard unit in 1968–69 has helped persuade him that the use of non-Regular troops in circumstances where the highest degree of control and training are required is not a philosophy which would wisely be reintroduced into Britain.

A far more serious challenge to the TA of the 1920s and 1930s was the government's power of the purse. County Associations, jealous of their statutory authority and financial independence, found themselves at odds with the Treasury. Several aspects of this friction have never disappeared. In 1988 an official report gently observed that 'with all the pressures on the Defence Vote', it was easy for the requirements of the TA and 'the supporting structure of the TAVRAs ... to become blurred in the higher peacetime profile cast by the Regular Army'.[15] The tension reflects the lack of understanding by some Regular officers and civil servants of the work done by TAVRAs, much of it local and low profile, but nonetheless essential. 'It is the Associations and *only* the Associations that provide the supportive local environment in which our independent Reserve units can flourish', observed two Association chairmen in 1990.[16] This ignorance is often paralleled by misunderstandings within the TA itself. As a subaltern I thought the TAVRAs were useless; as a major I knew they were useful, and as a Commanding Officer I found them far more responsive to many of my day-to-day problems than my own (Regular) chain of command. The problem is compounded by the fact that as the purely military demands on TA officers have increased, at a time when, generally, the pressures of their 'day jobs' has also become more intense, they have less time to involve themselves in the workings of important TAVRA subcommittees which were bread and butter to officers of my generation.

Sometimes, too, the supporting fire delivered by TAVRAs at times of TA restructuring causes tension, especially as it ranges from telling, well-aimed shots at clearly identified targets (for an example of just how perceptive TAVRA support can be, see the evidence given to the House of Commons Defence Committee by Colonels Mike Taylor, Tony Sellon and Richard Putnam in December 1998[17]) and unhelpful bursts as likely to injure friend as foe: if I sound wounded, it is because I am. And it also reflects the fact that TAVRAs themselves have not always been user-friendly. I recall a senior official at the MOD animadverting, with an asperity heightened, I suspect, by what he regarded as unhelpful TAVRA forays into defence politics, that their accounting did not mesh comfortably with best modern practice. The independent status of individual TAVRAs (themselves amalgamations of the old County Committees for whom independence was a deliberate element of Haldane's original intent) means that they have to be led, exhorted and cajoled rather than controlled: I am struck by the analogy of herding cats. Significantly, the London-based Council of TAVRAs is their servant, not their master. The quality of the full-time secretaries/chief executives of individual associations – and I speak, *bien sûr*, of the past – has not been consistent. They are retired Regular officers, sometimes the ex-commander of the local Regional Brigade. I have occasionally been struck by facility with which some of these gallant gentlemen, having seen little of the TA during their Regular careers, emerge as its strongest supporters and tell me how little I understand it, or how I am in danger of 'selling out to the Regulars'. Finally, over the past few years it has been impossible not to sense tension between Harris tweed and Hugo Boss, with the waning power of the old county connections set against the growing strength of the Whitehall apparat. During the debate over the SDR someone observed that 'the Lords Lieutenant would never stand it'. I am not sure that the Lords Lieutenant cut quite the ice with George Robertson that they did with R. B. Haldane.

Perhaps the most serious comparison between the difficulties of the inter-war years and those of the recent past was the simple fact that the Regular army and the TA were forced to compete for their share of a defence budget which was itself under pressure. This has often been more a matter of cruel necessity than active malice. In 1922 the Earl of Scarborough observed:

> "From my experience of the Military Members of the Army Council I have little doubt that they would welcome abolition [of the Territorial Army] and if thereby they can save something substantial for the Regular Army they will probably press for it, and if successful destroy the one thing that keeps the voluntary spirit alive in the Country."[18]

The noble lord was close to the truth, for a War Office conference of regional commanders earlier that year had already concluded that the ten year rule – which decreed that military planning would proceed on the basis that there would be no major war for the next ten years – meant that the TA 'fulfils none of the essential tasks which the maintenance of the British Empire demands. On the contrary, it is absorbing money to fund which regular units are to be abolished. It is impossible, therefore, to justify the retention of the Territorial Army in its present form on military grounds.'[19]

The TA was cut but not abolished, with familiar measures like the reduction of unit establishments, recruit capping even within these establishments, and the reductions of the regular permanent staff of TA units all helping to reduce its cost. The damage would undoubtedly have been worse without the TA's powerful political constituency, and the realisation, hinted at in even in the War Office conference report, that the TA had implications that were not purely military. It contributed to social cohesion, and helped men from the economically depressed areas of the United Kingdom find part-time occupation which made them feel valued and valuable. Examination of the location of the annual camps attended by TA units in the inter-war years suggests that the process went much farther. Camps were often in or near seaside resorts; Territorials sometimes took their families, which put up at boarding houses, and the training programme was not so rigorous as to prevent the atmosphere being a strange hybrid of training camp and seaside holiday. Small wonder that when the GOC 42nd (East Lancashire) Division pointed out that 'a holiday by the seaside was of no benefit to training' he found himself supported neither by his county association (which cannot have surprised him) nor by the Commanding Officers of his own units.[20] The Ministry of Labour's profoundly unsympathetic interpretation of regulations for the grant of public assistance to unemployed Territorials, however, was little short of scandalous, and many Territorial Commanding Officers found themselves wrestling with problems which were more socio-economic than military. It was only when the danger of a rearming Germany was unmistakably clear that the government at last made serious preparations to meet it. Amongst them was the doubling of the TA, announced in March 1939. The measure was stunningly ill-advised. The turbulence it injected into the TA took years to subside, and the poor performance of some TA divisions in France in 1940 bears eloquent testimony to the folly of expecting brave men to make up for years of neglect.

The experience of the TA in the inter-war years does provide us with the glint of a distant mirror. One of the underlying assumptions behind the 1998 Strategic Defence Review was that Britain would not face a major threat to her direct national security in the short to medium term, and that the political warning of a growing threat, perhaps from a resurgent Russia, would trigger military reaction time in which the appropriate preparations could be made. It is hard to quibble with this fundamental logic – just as it would have been hard to disagree with the inter-war Ten Year Rule when it was first adopted in 1919. But the Ten Year Rule outlived its usefulness, and history suggests that it is no simple matter to identify risks while they are still over the horizon, and to ensure that taxpayers recognise why money should be devoted to military preparations before intangible risks have become real and present threats. We must not assume that democratic politicians in the early 21st century will make the same mistake as their forefathers in the 1920s and 1930s, but the evidence of the past suggests that a system which reacted so slowly to the resurgence of Germany in the 1930s requires brave and perceptive management. Nor should we forget that in the more recent past there have been campaigns, like that in the Falklands in 1982 and the Gulf in 1990–91, which caught the defence establishment at a disadvantage. A recent, notably irreverent, Assistant Chief of the General Staff had in his office a framed compendium of comments from policy-making civil servants asking what possible justification there was for believing that Britain would ever fight east of Suez or send tanks to the Middle East.

Warning is valuable only inasmuch as it provides time in which to do something useful. The very long procurement time of many modern weapons systems and, relatively long procurement time of some natures of ammunition, must give cause for concern. So too must the time it takes to increase the size of armed forces. This is not just a matter of raising, training and equipping men (and, increasingly, women), though, as the experience of the British army at the beginning of two world wars demonstrates, the raising of mass armies from a society with no deep-seated tradition of conscription inevitably dilutes quality. At least part of the reason for the flat spots in British military performance in 1915–16 and 1940–42 is the hasty raising of troops who were committed to battle before they were ready. As far as the Second World War is concerned, Field Marshal Montgomery's much-quoted comment that the British army was 'totally unfit to fight a first class war on the continent of Europe' has the ring of truth.[21] But an arguably more serious matter is the question of generating and maintaining popular support for the business of expansion, especially in a society as demilitarised as that in contemporary Britain, where the decreasing size of armed forces – Regular and Reserve – means that fewer and fewer people will come into contact with a serviceman. Ours is a society where few know the difference between a brigadier and a bombardier, and Regulars are judged by the television series *Soldier, Soldier* and Territorials by *All Quiet on the Preston Front*. Antony Beevor's *Inside the British Army* depicted a force dismayed at the quality of its recruits: 'They are not necessarily insubordinate, one sergeant explained, they just don't know what authority or rank mean.'[22] Defence, as a political issue, pales into insignificance before health and education. Although the services retain a high level of public approval, the problems associated with the military's 'need to be different' have, as Christopher Dandeker has observed, moved centre-stage in recent years.[23] Assumptions about the practicality of raising forces – of whatever sort – in this climate should not be made lightly, and though the SDR did indeed articulate the role of Reserve Forces (who often constitute the only military presence in many areas) in this respect, the diminution of the Reserve Force footprint remains one significant criticism of the review.[24]

After the outbreak of the Second World War the Territorial Army lost its separate identity, and Regular and Territorial armies merged in a single force. TA officers removed the letter T from below their badges of rank, although in one unit they responded to their regular adjutant's congratulation that they were now spared the stigma by wearing them invisibly under their pocket flaps to make the point that being Territorials was a source of pride. The TA was not re-established immediately after the war, but during the late 1940s it reassumed its familiar guise with regional divisions, trained and equipped to fight as such, composed of genuine volunteers and as well as National Servicemen who retained an obligation to serve in the TA after their full-time service ended.

By the mid-1960s the system was past its best. John Baynes,

then Regular Brigade Major of a TA Infantry Brigade, thought that the TA 'under-funded, under-recruited in most units ... with its 20-year-old, wartime weapons and equipment', was due for a shake-up.[25] The TA I joined as a private soldier in 1964 was all too evidently under-equipped and under-manned. Although the presence of many officers and NCOs with Second World War medal ribbons and the extraordinary sense of camaraderie were alike impressive, the unsympathetic suggestion that it was a drinking-club in which pay – then given in cash – was instantly converted into beer in the battery canteen strikes a chord with my own experience. Its divisional structure was increasingly perceived as being inappropriate to Britain's real security needs. In 1962 a Territorial Army Emergency Reserve – 'the Ever Readies' – with a much greater liability for overseas service was instituted in an effort to make the force more usable in the 'brushfire wars' of the era, and in 1965 some Territorials were mobilised for service in Aden. However, the Ever Ready experiment was not a success, in part because some of its members regarded the then substantial bounty of £150 as 'money for old rope' and its effect upon units, which included a minority of Ever Readies as well as Territorials on normal terms of service, was deeply divisive.[26]

The TA restructuring of 1967 was radical indeed. It combined the TA and the much smaller Army Emergency Reserve, itself the descendent of the old Special Reserve, and its name changed to the unloved Territorial and Army Volunteer Reserve (T&AVR), divided into four categories, the first two of which (the Volunteers) enjoyed the best training and equipment. T&AVR III (the Territorials), had less glamorous roles, and were first reduced to soldiering without pay – the fact that they did so speaks volumes for the morale of the old TA, whatever its limitations in training or efficiency – and then reduced to cadres. After the return of a Conservative government in 1979 the TA's old name was speedily restored, and there was increasing use of the expression 'One Army' to emphasise the essential unity (albeit subsuming a natural diversity!) of the army's Regular and Territorial elements within a single chain of command. The TA was gradually increased, first by the addition of what became known to some as 'Heath battalions' after the Prime

Minister of the day. These were home defence units on lighter scales of equipment than the existing NATO-roled units. It is worth noting that these new units generally took several years to establish themselves fully, emphasising the real difficulty of expanding the TA on what was, of necessity, a narrow training base, despite robust government support which increased the TA's establishment from 59,000 in 1979 to a planned 'Phase Two Enhancement' figure of 86,000 in 1990.[27]

It is also striking that TA strength failed to attain its new establishment figure, pointing to a consistent under-recruiting factor. In December 1992 a parliamentary debate suggested that although establishment (which then included the Home Service Force) was 91,000, strength was 74,000, and perhaps 63,000 to 65,000 trained regularly.[28] Except when downsizing to reach a new, smaller establishment, the TA's strength seldom attains its establishment figure, and I have grave doubts whether the post-SDR establishment of 41,200 will be any different in this respect. The reasons for this are numerous, but chief amongst them is arguably the fact that TA strength reflects the size of its national footprint, and the reduction of this footprint reduces recruiting potential. There are always a few zealots who drive long distances (Geoff Fairfax, my own redoubtable Company Sergeant Major, regularly drove from Broadstairs to Guildford for training nights and weekends) but the majority travel less than ten miles from home to TA centre. And it must be said that the publicity campaign waged by the TA's supporters *before* successive restructuring tends to have baneful effects *after* them. The public, having been told vociferously that the TA is under threat, is then too easily persuaded that it has indeed been disbanded. My own TA career has been punctuated by surprise expressed by my non-military friends that there was still a TA left to serve in. Tabloid headlines are no help: the SDR restructuring, which, as we shall see, left a respectably-sized TA, was greeted with the daft epitaph 'Ta Ta, TA.'

The establishment of TA of the 1990s sank back from heights of the Phase 2 enhancement figure, firstly as a result of Options for Change and then of the Defence Costs Study. It was not simply numbers that were reduced, but, as the House of Commons Defence Committee Report on Options noted, 'the relatively harsh treatment of the infantry is indicative of the strategic transformation of the TA towards combat support and away from "teeth" arms.'[29] But with the reductions in numbers and shift in emphasis came an unmistakable sign of change in focus. Although reservists, regular and volunteer, were used in the Gulf War, the war showed that it was difficult to gain access to the categories of reserves needed for such Out of Area Operations. In March 1992 the MOD announced the results of a study into the Regular/Reserve mix, carried out in the aftermath of the Gulf War, and declared that 'there is seen to be a greater need for Reserves to support our regular forces at relatively short notice in lower levels of conflict', and noted that there needed to be 'significant changes' in the legislative framework governing the use of reserves.[30] Eighteen months later the Ministry reiterated its intention (emphasis in original) to '*plan also to use the capabilities of the Reserves in two ways in circumstances short of major war*'.[31] This would include the use of reservists in specialist capacities for which there was little need in peacetime, and, more significantly, to 'supplement the existing Regular capability on a broader front to meet temporary increases in commitments'.[32]

The new legislative framework was set out in RFA 96, the result of a lengthy consultative process outside the MOD, and of internal deliberations in which legally-qualified reservists were themselves involved.[33] Nicholas Soames, then Minister of State for the Armed Forces, set out the deficiencies of the previous legislation in 1994, arguing that it did not apply to all Reserves, was inconsistent, failed to allow for call-out of the Reserves in precisely those circumstances where their use, in the New World Order, was most desirable, and imposed substantial practical difficulties in the use to which Reservists could be put without formal call-out. Members of a TA platoon sent to the Falklands, for instance, had been forced to leave the TA and become short-term regulars.[34]

Amongst other provisions, the new legislation, which attracted wide all-party support, widened the circumstances under which reservists could be called out, and enabled them to serve on Full-Time Reserve Service. Serving reservists had either to elect to be bound by the new law or became liable to it when they re-enlisted or were commissioned, and the overwhelming majority of reservists are now so bound. Those who are not – 'Transitional members' – include a number of officers who fear that the widening of call-out conditions to include operations for the protection of life or property at home and abroad would pose an unacceptable risk to their civilian careers. No individuals have yet been compulsorily mobilised without their consent under RFA 96: those sent to the Balkans and elsewhere have been asked to volunteer and, having done so, are then mobilised. However, in the early summer of 1999 a large-scale mobilisation under RFA 96 was averted only by Serbia's decision to withdraw from Kosovo.

The debate within the TA over the implementation of RFA 96 became subsumed in the broader issue of the SDR. In a sense the latter simply continued the logic of the TA downsizing carried out by the previous administration, emphasising that Reserves would be used as required, with compulsion taking place if it proved impossible to rely on sufficient reservists volunteering. The Labour government was disarmingly frank: 'Selective compulsory call-out is therefore envisaged for situations well short of a direct threat to the United Kingdom – for example, for deployments on a similar scale to the Gulf war.' It added that reservists 'must be available and expect to be mobilised under the 1996 Reserve Forces Act. We will be emphasising to our volunteers the seriousness of their responsibilities in this regard.'[35]

The SDR reduced the TA to an establishment of 41,200, and the changes that it made in the combat arms caused particular grief, occasioning, as they did, the disbandment of all but one of the TA battalions of regular regiments in favour of companies, affiliated by cap-badge to regular regiments, grouped within wide-spread TA battalions. It is too early to be absolutely sure whether the new TA is survivable in terms of footprint and overall critical mass, and restructuring certainly proved the last straw for many whose commitment had already been eroded by changes under the previous administration. The TA has always provided substantial support to the cadet movement – which itself has much social merit – and although this aspect of the footprint was very seriously considered by ministers, I am concerned that the cadets may suffer because of TA restructuring. A senior Territorial suggested to me that while a TA of 45,000 would have represented a heavy landing, with few breakages, one of

40,000 represented a crash landing, with some fatalities, and in my judgement he was right. Bruce George, the robust chairman of the House of Commons Defence Committee, detected 'an undercurrent of distrust, and, on occasion, disdain from some sections of the Regular Army and MOD when dealing with the TA ...' and emphasised that his committee would require the MOD 'to prove to us that they have delivered on their promises'.[36] What seems clear, however, is that the restructured TA, despite the grief over disbandments, infantry establishments which still seem too taut, medical aspirations which will take many years to realise, spans of command which may be too wide and a footprint which is almost certainly too narrow, is within the ball park of survivability: though the detail might not yet be right, the principle is. I supported it when Director of Reserve Forces and Cadets, not because my job depended on it – one of the luxuries of being a Territorial is that resignation on a point of principle rarely poses an economic problem – but because it was not a bad deal, and was not far short of being a good one.

However, RFA 96 and the SDR between them represent a break with the Haldane tradition. The TA is no longer what it has been for much of its history, a force designed to fight a major war against an adversary who can be identified, with some confidence, in advance. In future its members – like the Special Reservists of 1908–14 and members of the post-Second World War AER – will tend to move closer to the Regular soldiers with whom they will do more and more business, and must recognise that they have more chance of being mobilised as individuals or sub-units than as units. The available evidence, patchy though it is, suggests that most Territorials accept this. A 1998 questionnaire-based study by Lieutenant Colonel Will Townend, a Regular officer who had commanded a TA unit, reported that 'if ordered, over 85% would respond to call-up for all types of operation without question', while 69% would consider volunteering a short period of full-time service, for example in Bosnia or Northern Ireland.[37]

Given the lack of wider statistical evidence we tend to rely on anecdote filtered through subjectivity. However, even with this caveat, I am persuaded that the vast majority of Territorials take the view of a lance corporal cited in the Townend study: 'If I'm ordered then of course I'll go: that's what I signed up for.' It seems to me that using the TA will not simply strengthen its whole *raison d'être* in both MOD politics (thus minimising the dangers of the marginalisation of the 1920s) and the wider community, but will encourage those who, like another of Townend's respondents, believe that: 'That's what we're here for.'[38] In January 2000 John Spellar, Minister of State for the Armed Forces, announced that a feasibility study on the use of the TA to sustain peace support operations in the Balkans had concluded that it was 'feasible in both legal and practical terms', and would be kept 'under constant review in the light of the prevailing operational conditions'.[39]

I believe that this reflects majority opinion within the Reserves, although there will be some towards the more settled side of the broad church comprising Reserve membership who may wish to reconsider their position. They should not, however, expect the nation to maintain an insurance policy upon which it had no intention of making a claim. There are also those who argue, like Sir Timothy Garden in a March 2000 article in *The Independent*, that the public expects wars to be fought by professionals, and that the Chief of Defence Staff's admission to the House of Commons Defence Committee that a forced entry into Kosovo would have required a substantial reserve mobilisation flew in the face of this logic.[40] Not so. While the public might expect the services, to 'live of their own' and cope without compulsory mobilisation of reservists in normal times, it would surely expect them, like any prudent business, to have mechanisms to cope with unexpected surges, and a major NATO warlike operation in the Balkans is surely such a surge. The converse, maintaining expensive regular forces (even if the recruits were available) to meet ill-defined eventualities, is far less likely to commend itself to taxpayers.

The Townend study identified job security as the main concern, noting that 'although most are aware of the protection given by RFA 96, they remain to be convinced that it will be upheld'.[41] The question of employer liaison remains of fundamental importance, Although the National Employers' Liaison Committee (NELC), established after a 1985 report suggested that difficulties with employers represented a major cause of TA wastage, has done well to establish a raft of supportive employers, more work needs to be done with small and medium sized employers and at the line management level of large supportive employers. It is clear that local Employer Liaison Committees, working to NELC and RFCAs, have a key role in the process. RFA 96 not only gives reservists the right to appeal to a Reserve Force Appeals Tribunal to obtain exemption or deferral from call-out, but extends the same right to employers. The MOD recognises that it should not attempt to ambush employers on mobilisation, but must take them into what the current NELC literature defines as 'A Profitable Partnership'. At the time of writing it seemed that the MOD might possibly be able to quantify the risk run by employers by undertaking – grave national emergencies apart, when all bets would be off – not to seek to mobilise an individual for longer than around six months, and not to revisit the same unit more than once in a five year period. It is evident from work done by NELC that the greater the warning time given to employers the more easily they will be able to cope with mobilisation, and Reservists and their employers alike have emphasised that compulsory mobilisation must be hung upon a solid operational peg, and not simply reflect undermanning in the Regular army.

Over 4,000 Reservists, most of them members of the TA, have served in Bosnia since 1995. They have ranged in rank from colonel to private, and in function from railway engineers to riflemen. In 1999 Commander Royal Engineers in Kosovo was a Territorial, whose mix of civilian qualifications and military experience made him ideal for the job. The army's record system still fails to capture the civilian specialisms of Territorials – my own records reveal that I can command a mortar platoon or an infantry company, but not that I can write film scripts or present TV documentaries – and sometimes it is the unexpected specialism that adds icing to the cake. A clerk in the Adjutant General's Corps rewired a small town, and a lance-corporal in the Green Howards deployed his skills as a stone-mason to good effect. There have been some failures, often when individuals arrived to do jobs for which they were ill-prepared, but far more successes. In the early years difficulties centred on pay and administration, and often reflected the unfamiliarity of Regular staff with the different procedures used by the TA. The establishment, on 1 April 1999, of the Reserves Training and Mobilisation Centre (RTMC) at Chillwell, near Nottingham, has made a palpable difference to both administration and attitude: reservists who experienced the old system of temporary mobilisation centres and have subsequently been mobilised through RTMC emphasise the superiority of the new system.

We are well on our way through the straits between the rock and the whirlpool, though it is anything but an easy cruise. However, as our course stands I believe that we will emerge with a TA which is more closely integrated into the British Army as a whole than has ever been the case in peacetime. But it would not take much to shatter our little craft, and I sometimes wonder if those on the quarter-deck know just how steamy life in the engine room really is. Ring up the telegraph for too many revolutions and the boiler may burst; yet ask the engines to idle and the stokers will lose interest. And do not take the morale of the crew for granted: this has been a very stormy voyage.

NOTES

1. Colin S. Gray, 'The American Revolution in Military Affairs: An Interim Assessment', *The Occasional* No. 28 (Strategic and Combat Studies Institute, Camberley, 1997) p. 10
2. 'A Study into the Relationship between the Regular Services and the Territorial, Auxiliary and Volunteer Reserve Associations (TAVRAs)' (The Chiswell Report) 25 August 1988, p. 2
3. Maj. Gen. Murray Naylor, 'The Challenge of the 90s for the Territorial Army', *RUSI Journal*, Vol. 137, No. 4, August 1992 p. 17.
4. Lt. Col. C.J.R. Day 'Making Sense of the Territorial Army' *RUSI Journal*, Vol. 137, No. 5, October 1992 p. 34.
5. Ibid. p. 38
6. Ibid.
7. Peter Dennis, *The Territorial Army 1907–1940* (Woodbridge, Suffolk 1987) p. 8. The best general study of British auxiliary forces remains Ian F. W. Beckett, *The Amateur Military Tradition, 1558–1945* (Manchester 1991).
8. Stanley Simm Baldwin, *Forward Everywhere: Her Majesty's Territorials* (London 1994).
9. See Ian F.W. Beckett, *Riflemen Form: A Study of the Rifle Volunteer Movement, 1859–1908* (Aldershot 1982).
10. George Ashurst, *My Bit: A Lancashire Fusilier at War, 1914–18* (Ramsbury, Wiltshire, 1987) pp. 24–5.
11. Dennis op.cit. p. 30.

12. Ibid. p. 32.
13. Quoted in Peter Caddick-Adams, *By God They Can Fight: A History of 143 Infantry Brigade 1908 to 1995* (Shrewsbury 1995) p. 67.
14. Dennis op.cit. pp. 60–61.
15. Chiswell Report p. 12.
16. Col. M.S. Lee-Brown and Col. T.L. May 'The TAVRAs', *British Army Review* August 1990, p. 39.
17. House of Commons Defence Committee 'The Strategic Defence Review: Territorial Army Restructuring', Minutes of Evidence 2 December 1998.
18. Scarborough to Churchill, 17 January 1922, quoted Dennis op.cit. p. 83
19. Minutes of War Office Conference of GOC-in-Cs, 3 January 1922, quoted ibid. p. 95.
20. Ibid. p. 150.
21. Quoted in Carlo d'Este 'The Army and the Challenge of War' in David Chandler and Ian Beckett (eds.) *The Oxford Illustrated History of the British Army* (Oxford 1994).
22. Anthony Beevor, *Inside the British Army* (London 1990) p. xxi.
23. Christopher Dandeker, 'Recent Trends in Military Culture' in Hew Strachan (ed.) *The British Army: Manpower and Society into the Twenty-First Century* (London 2000) p. 174.
24. Strategic Defence Review: Supporting Essay seven, Reserve Forces, para 27.
25. John Baynes 'Recruiting the Professional Army 1960-1980' in Strachan op.cit. p. 52.
26. Baldwin op.cit. p. 169.
27. Defence Open Government Document 84/02 'Territorial Army Expansion 1986–1990.'
28. *Hansard*, 12 December 1991 Col. 1112.
29. House of Commons Defence Committee, 'Options for Change: Reserve Forces' (London 1992) p. xix.
30. 'The Future of Britain's Reserve Forces', Defence Open Government Document, March 1992.
31. 'Britain's Reserve Forces: A Framework for the Future', MOD October 1993 p. 5.
32. Ibid.
33. Lt. Col. M.E. Hatt-Cook 'The Reserve Forces Act 1995 [sic]' *RUSI Journal*, Vol. 138, No. 5, October 1993.
34. Nicholas Soames 'Towards New Reserve Forces Legislation', *RUSI Journal*, Vol. 139, No. 6, December 1994.
35. Strategic Defence Review, Supporting Essay Seven, Reserve Forces, paras 22–3.
36. Bruce George 'MPs fight a Rearguard Action for the TA', *RUSI Journal*, Vol. 144, No. 2, April/May 1999, pp. 23–4.
37. Lt. Col. W. A. H. Townend, 'Mobilisation in the Territorial Army of the Future', unpublished service fellowship dissertation, Harris Manchester College, Oxford, Michaelmas Term 1998, pp. 2–9.
38. Ibid. p. 28.
39. *Hansard*, 13 January 2000 Col. 208W.
40. *The Independent*, 17 March 2000.
41. Townend op.cit. p. 33.

6

Tri-Service Equal Opportunities Initiatives

RICHARD DOUGLAS
Tri-Service Equal Opportunities Training Centre

INTRODUCTION

A key element of the Strategic Defence Review was the emphasis on a 'Policy for People' and a recommendation that the Ministry of Defence should develop an Armed Forces Overarching Personnel Strategy (AFOPS). Such a policy was published in February 2000 with an overall statement setting out the Service personnel vision as follows:

> *'To generate and maintain, joint, battle winning forces, by placing Service personnel and their families at the centre of our plans, investing in them and giving them confidence in their future.'*[1]

The AFOPS details a number of Personnel Strategy Guidelines (PSGs) which provide the detail for the implementation of its 28 personnel policy areas. Personnel Strategy Guideline 15,[2] in detailing the Armed Forces Equal Opportunities Policy, builds on the extensive work that has already been undertaken and provides direction on the future development within this key personnel area. PSG 15 reflects the need for the Armed Forces to continue to recruit and retain high calibre personnel irrespective of race, ethnic origin, religion or gender and without reference to social background or sexual orientation. The ultimate aim being to enhance operational effectiveness.

Although led by the Ministry of Defence, PSG 15 is in keeping with extensive work being carried out across all government departments. Managing equality remains one of the government's top priorities and, in turn, the senior ministerial and military personnel within the MOD have decreed that the Armed Forces and Civil Service are to play a pivotal part in this. Indeed they want us to become a beacon of best practice for others.

> 'We are determined to see the Army, Navy, Royal Air Force and Civil Service more closely reflect the rich diversity of British society.' [3]

> 'The Armed Forces, like all good employers, recognise that to maintain their reputation as the best in the business, they need to attract the brightest people from all sections of society, irrespective of race and gender...it is common sense not political correctness.' [4]

The Royal Navy, Army and Royal Air Force have already undertaken a considerable amount of work in order to improve equality of opportunity and to ensure that all personnel have the chance to work in an environment free from harassment and intimidation. A Tri-Service corporate approach has been developed to take this work forward across the Armed Forces. This has involved the development of a Corporate Equal Opportunities Goal as follows:

> "The Services EO goal is to achieve universal acceptance and application of a working environment free from harassment, intimidation and unlawful discrimination, in which all have equal opportunity, consistent with our legal obligations, to realise their full potential in contributing to the maintenance and enhancement of operational effectiveness. The Armed Forces respect and value every individual's unique contribution, irrespective of their race, ethnic origin, religion or gender and without reference to social background or sexual orientation." [5]

This Goal is underpinned by the following five principles:

* All personnel will be accountable for the implementation of Service and civilian equality and diversity programmes.
* All harassment and unlawful discrimination will be challenged and action taken to address prejudice and negative attitudes.

- Complaints will be dealt with fairly and expeditiously.
- All equality policies will be monitored and evaluated.
- The composition of the Armed Forces should better reflect the society they exist to defend.

THE TRI-SERVICE EQUAL OPPORTUNITIES TRAINING CENTRE

As an integral element of turning Departmental policy into practice the Tri-Service Equal Opportunities Training Centre (TSEOTC) was established at Shrivenham in March 1998 as a centre of excellence to deliver specialist Equal Opportunities training. In the first two years of operation the Centre has trained in excess of 2000 personnel from all three Services and the MOD Civil Service. The training delivered by the Centre is designed to ensure that the requirement for each member of the Armed Forces to take responsibility for delivering full integration of equal opportunities into all working practices is fully understood. The training is part of a 'top-down, bottom-up' approach to equality management across the MOD with both Senior Officers and unit level EO Advisers receiving specific training packages.

TSEOTC is responsible for the delivery of one day Senior Officer Equal Opportunities Awareness Seminars and five-day Equal Opportunities Advisers Courses. Both courses are designed to produce informed debate around the myriad of emotive issues that are raised under the auspices of equal opportunities. Attendees on both courses receive background instruction on the appropriate national and European legislation as well as covering MOD policy on all the relevant issues. Of greater importance is the opportunity for all concerned to challenge their own attitudes and to consider how they can personally take responsibility for implementing the MOD 'Zero Tolerance' policy within their own area of influence. Both courses use an interactive learning approach with all students being actively involved. Whilst the level of instruction remains critical to the success of the training, the input provided by a Tri-Service student group is also important. Many students gain a great deal from discussion amongst themselves which helps to bring the subject matter to life in a meaningful manner.

Senior officer awareness seminars are mandatory for all 'One Star' (Brigadiers and equivalent) or grade 6 MoD Civil Servant and above. The seminar, entitled 'Leadership and Equality', aims to raise awareness of equal opportunities and diversity to enable all senior officers to discharge their important leadership role in promoting equal opportunities and diversity in the Armed Forces and MOD Civil Service. This one day course is delivered by external consultants – Domino Consultancy – who have much experience in developing and delivering EO training for both the public and private sector. It is an intensive and highly interactive day with the Commandant of the TSEOTC sitting in to provide a military input. Despite the mandatory nature of the training, the seminar continues to be well received. The course remains dynamic and is deliberately set into the context of the MOD. Comments such as "A worthwhile experience – despite initial scepticism" are frequently received. Debate during the training is far reaching but an acceptance of the need for consideration of all the issues is widespread. The following quotes are from recent attendees on the course and confirm the relevance of the training to the Armed Forces:

> "We have the legal right to use violent force. The officer corps has to know when and how to use violent force therefore we must be 'civilised'. Officers must know how to manage violent force."

> "People need to have regard to their responsibilities rather than their rights."

Every unit, establishment or formation HQ in the three Services is required to appoint an Equal Opportunities Adviser (EOA). The five-day EOA course at TSEOTC is designed to prepare those nominated for the EOA role with the knowledge, skills and attributes to carry out the task. The role of the Equal Opportunities Adviser is to advise the Commanding Officer, and all unit personnel (military and civilian), on the full spectrum of EO issues. They may also be required to run equal opportunities training. The five-day EOA course covers both the theoretical principles and practical implementation of the Armed Forces corporate approach, and the single Service policies on equal opportunities. Students are given a clear understanding of discrimination, harassment and bullying through discussion of real case studies and personal experiences. Additionally they have an opportunity to explore their own attitudes and prejudices, and to understand how these can lead to discriminatory behaviour. Students also benefit from the opportunity to role play a number of situations involving potentially sensitive EO issues and to practice the delivery of training on relevant, and often highly emotive, issues. The course includes practical sessions on how to implement the policies within their own units. Those attending the course usually fall within the rank range of Warrant Officer to Major although a significant number of Lieutenant Colonels have also attended.

Prior to establishing both the Tri Service Equal Opportunities Training Centre and the Equal Opportunities Advisers Course a project officer, Lieutenant Colonel (now Colonel) Isobel McCord,[6] was appointed to undertake extensive research in order to establish best practice. In conjunction with staff from the Service Personnel Policy branch in MOD she considered the work of a number of other agencies in the private and public sectors. This included consideration of the work already being undertaken by other Armed Forces The research confirmed that a policy of zero tolerance of all forms of harassment, discrimination and bullying is in direct support of the Defence Mission; a mission which lists as its highest critical factor for achieving success the ability to recruit and retain the best people for the job from a diverse society. Consequently, the training courses that were developed from Colonel McCord's work have been designed to show that equal opportunities is an issue which includes everyone not just the perceived minority groups. Enshrined within these courses is the principle that through good leadership and management everyone is responsible for ensuring that attitudes are challenged and unacceptable behaviour is changed. The ability of the course to achieve this is highlighted in the following comment received from an Army Warrant Officer at the end of his five-day course:

'In my sordid past; I have been the bully, been bullied; harassed soldiers and been harassed; I have upheld the law whilst breaking it myself and most strikingly; I have been ignorant through a placid attitude. We all need to know what is going on and I believe that this is why I *needed* this course. By coming on this week, I have realised where I came from, what I did wrong and can now make a difference.'

At both Senior Officer and Equal Opportunities Adviser level the training is designed to show that Equal Opportunities and Diversity Management within the MOD are not about being politically correct but are about:

• Fair and decent behaviour for everyone, both the majority and minority.
• Valuing differences rather than treating everyone the same – diversity management.
• An essential part of good leadership and management.

CONCLUSIONS

The Armed Forces need to recruit and retain high calibre individuals, irrespective of their race, ethnic origin, religion, gender, sexual orientation or social background. This is fundamental to improving operational effectiveness, as is the creation of a culture in which all individuals are valued for their contribution. Promotion of equality of opportunity is therefore of primary importance to the Armed Forces. The Services Equal Opportunities goal is to achieve universal acceptance and application of a working environment free from harassment, intimidation and unlawful discrimination, in which all have equal opportunity, consistent with our legal obligations, to realise their full potential in contributing to the maintenance and enhancement of operational effectiveness. The Armed Forces value every single individual member of the MOD – be they Service or Civilian, black or white, male or female, heterosexual or homosexual. To value them not because it is politically correct to do so but because without a working environment which encourages them to contribute fully to the operational efficiency of their section, squadron, ship or unit at whatever level, our collective ability to meet the Defence Mission will be continually eroded. It is that simple fact that justifies why a policy of zero tolerance of discrimination, harassment and bullying at all levels is a key component in enhancing operational effectiveness.

Progress within the past two years has been considerable although the continuing appearance of adverse comment within the press leaves us in no doubt that more can be achieved in this highly emotive and dynamic subject area. The MOD entered into partnership with the Commission For Racial Equality at a time when comments such as the one below were the norm:

> *'If there had been a booby prize for the major employer with the least commitment to equality of opportunity, then, in the past, the Ministry of Defence would surely have been favourite to win.'* [7]

So, it is a measure of how far policy and practice within all three Services has progressed that public recognition is now visible in many areas. This is epitomised by the following quotation from Sir Herman Ouseley, then Chair of the Commission for Racial Equality

> *"The Armed Forces have recognised that equality and diversity are positive strengths for an organisation and their work in this area is setting standards that other sections of society should follow."* [8]

NOTES

1. Ministry of Defence. *Armed Forces Overarching Personnel Strategy.* February 2000. (See Foreword by G. Hoon Secretary of State for Defence).
2. Ibid. p. 44.
3. Ministry of Defence. *Defence White Paper. Cm. 4446.* December 1999.
4. General Sir Charles Guthrie, speech at the Royal Society of Arts Conference "Learning from Experience." 10 November 1998.
5. Defence Council Instruction/Joint Service 22/00.
6. She later became the first Commandant of the TSEOC
7. *The Independent,* 31 March 1998.
8. Sir Herman Ouseley, Chairman of CRE. "Into Leadership" Conference. June 1999.

7

Managing Ethnic Minority Recruitment in the Uniformed Services: A Scottish Perspective

ASIFA HUSSAIN

Scottish Centre for War Studies, University of Glasgow

INTRODUCTION

Very little is known about ethnic recruitment into the uniformed services in the United Kingdom. Much of this ignorance is due to the lack of research in this area, and the subsequent scarcity of relevant literature. This chapter aims to rekindle interest in this under researched area. In addition, the relevance of this chapter is vindicated by a Home Office report[1] published in July 1999, highlighting the situation regarding ethnic minorities in the uniformed services, and in particular the repeated calls by government ministers to redress the poor ethnic minority representation in public sector organisations.[2]

Essentially, this chapter looks at four representatives of the uniformed services in Scotland – the prison, police, fire and armed services – that are trying to boost ethnic minority recruitment into their ranks. In order to meet this objective they have established the Uniformed Services' Committee. This chapter shows that the Uniformed Services' Committee have set the standards and led the way in Scotland by putting into place mechanisms to boost ethnic minority recruitment. Furthermore, since the committee was formed before the publication of the Home Office report that stressed the need to address the low level of ethnic minority recruitment in selected public-sector uniformed services on a national scale, this demonstrates considerable resourcefulness on the part of the Scottish services. There is scope for such an approach to be applied across the whole country, on a national basis. The Scottish Uniformed Services' Committee represents a unique development and is an example of good practice. Naturally it will take time before it will be able to make an appreciable impact. However, the committee represents a significant coup for Scotland, especially appropriate in light of the increasing publicity and attention the country has received since the inauguration of the Scottish Parliament. The lesson for the rest of the country to follow is that there is a framework in place, encompassing both effectiveness and efficiency.

To facilitate its goals, this chapter is divided into a number of sections which cover the following: an overview of the methodology which underpins this research; a review of some of the key literature which has covered the issue of discrimination and recruitment of minorities in the public sector; some background as to how the twin issues of racism and ethnic minority recruitment have resurfaced in recent years in public sector organisations, and the impetus that these gave to the evolution of the Uniformed Services' Committee; and an assessment of the recruitment potential of the different services through an examination of the methods and strategies used to tackle the recruitment problem by the various Scottish uniformed services.

METHODOLOGICAL APPROACH

This chapter draws on a rich source of primary material, including statistical data from official bodies, government documents, and interviews and meetings with key figures in the different uniformed services. A total of seven semi-structured interviews were conducted with officials representing the various services, and these interviews provide a very useful insight into the current predicament facing the services which make up the Uniformed Services' Committee. The questions put to interviewees were deliberately open-ended in the hope that this would entice their general feelings on the issue at hand. Interviews were conducted with individuals representing the following services in Scotland: the Royal Navy; the Army; the Royal Air Force; the Prison Service; the Strathclyde Police and the Scottish Fire Brigade. In addition, attendance at meetings of the Uniformed Services' Committee provided the author with an insight into the committee's aspirations and its activities.

SUMMARY OF LITERATURE

The literature on ethnic minority recruitment has covered in small doses various public sector organisations such as education, health, the police and the judicial system.[3] The different works have shown that ethnic minorities have suffered racial discrimination in the recruitment process and promotion system and physical and verbal racial abuse which has impeded their recruitment and forced existing ones to leave, thus creating a retention as well as recruitment problem. Furthermore, they have shown that racism has not featured heavily on the agenda of uniformed organisations because of the failure to acknowledge it as a problem and a lack of motivation to pursue equal opportunities, taking advantage of the immunity from the Race Relations Act 1976 which the police and National Health Service (NHS) have enjoyed.[4]

Existing studies already provide ample proof that institutions where racism exists are unable to attract ethnic minorities in numbers that are deemed sufficient. Two good examples being the police and NHS. Fielding[5] in his study of the police notes the way in which the 'culture' of the police has inhibited the recruitment and career advancement of ethnic minority officers. This is a problem that is equally applicable to the armed services, where service culture, characterised by discrimination and stereotyping, has played a key role in both the failure to attract ethnic minorities and to retain existing ones. Beishon[6] notes a similar development in the NHS where organisational barriers related to the internal culture of the NHS have dissuaded ethnic minorities from seeking employment in the NHS. Sheffield and Hussain[7] reviewed the institutional racism encountered by ethnic minorities in the NHS seeking promotion and equal treatment. They found that widespread racism encountered by ethnic minority staff was inhibiting both the recruitment of ethnic minorities and the retention of existing ones, thereby compounding the current staffing crisis, a view backed in turn by Abbott.[8]

As studies of the NHS and police have highlighted, the persistence of racial discrimination in public sector organisations over a period of time is witness to the failure of the organisational system to stamp it out. A number of factors have contributed to this. One of these has been organisational blindness, the inability of organisations to accept racism as a problem, perhaps because it has become heavily embedded in the culture of the organisation. In addition there has been an ineffective system of checks and balances in organisations, and not enough resources being targeted to tackle the problem. The burden of responsibility has to be with management, which has the power to effect change or at least trigger the process. In the case of the armed forces, the MoD, after many years, acknowledged the problem of being blind to racism, and has now instituted measures to redress this shortcoming.

According to Liff and Dickens[9] what may help organisations to take equality on board are not just the arguments based on social justice or morality but to what has become known as the 'business case strategy', where positive organisational benefits of equal opportunity can be seen from the point of view of "pragmatic self-interest", with employers recognising that the adoption of equality measures can serve their interests in competing in the labour market, enhance organisational performance and service delivery.

PROLIFERATION OF THE DEBATE ON RACE AND RECRUITMENT AND THE EMERGENCE OF THE UNIFORMED SERVICES' COMMITTEE

The condensed definition of institutional racism forwarded by Sir William Macpherson is "the collective failure of an organisation to provide an appropriate and professional service to people because of their colour, culture or ethnic origin. It can be seen, or detected in processes, attitudes, thoughtlessness and racist stereotyping which disadvantages minority ethnic groups."[10] Racism has been a problem which has afflicted more than one uniformed service and public sector institution.[11] Indeed, after the Lawrence Inquiry, the Commission for Racial Equality conceded that the police service is not the only organisation within society, which has problems of racism.[12] The armed forces, especially, have been strongly criticised for racism within their ranks. A report by the Office for Public Management divulged findings that racism was salient across all three services.[13] The racial experiences encountered by Sergeant Jacob Malcolm (who was barred from joining the Household Cavalry because of his colour) Private Stephen Anderson and Richard Stokes, led to the implementation of a five-year action plan under the auspices of the Commission for Racial Equality,[14] which aimed to tackle discriminatory attitudes and behaviour.[15] This commitment by the Ministry of Defence in alleviating the problem and making change has not gone unnoticed. In 1998, the Commission for Racial Equality lifted the threat of a formal non-discrimination notice under the Race Relations Act.[16]

The police have constantly been the subject of scrutiny in the media. The most recent major incidence being the Stephen Lawrence case, where a youth of Afro-Caribbean descent was killed by white youths and whose death left behind a trail of injustice as a result of a bungled police investigation into his murder.[17] The report by Sir William Macpherson described racism as being severe in the Metropolitan Police: "pernicious and institutionalised".[18] It provided the Metropolitan Police with 70 recommendations.

In the prison service there have also been reports of racial bullying by white inmates towards ethnic minority prison officers, and by white prison officers towards black and Asian prisoners.

Table 1 (p.118) shows that ethnic minority representation in the uniformed services, which have all been criticised for being racist, is considerably below 7%, the proportion of the UK population which is classed as being of ethnic origin. The Home Office Report[19] into ethnic minority representation details an action plan to remedy this problem. However, similar aims were adopted by the Uniformed Services' Committee in Scotland well before the Report's publication, showing the initiative that the Scottish region has shown in instigating its own strategy, prior to any central government prompting. It has to be pointed out that the figures in Table 1 are national statistics, there are no separate figures available for the Scottish uniformed services. It is clear though, that in Scotland minority representation in each of the services is also below the proportion of the Scottish population which is of ethnic origin, otherwise these services would not have formed the Uniformed Services' Committee, as there would not have been a major need for it.

TABLE 1
NATIONAL (UK) ETHNIC MINORITY REPRESENTATION IN SELECTED
UNIFORMED SERVICES

Service	Current Ethnic Minority Representation
Armed Forces	1.1%
Prison	3.2%
Police	3.0%
Fire	1.2%

Source: Home Office.

For some years now, the uniformed services in Scotland have collectively been exploring various ways of recruiting ethnic minorities into the services. One outcome was the creation of the Uniformed Services' Committee, incorporating the armed forces, police, prison and fire services. Glasgow was chosen as the headquarters of the committee because it is the largest and most populated city in Scotland, and occupies the central belt of Scotland where the majority of the Scottish population lives, and where most of Scotland's 1.3% ethnic minorities reside. The ideology behind the Uniformed Services' Committee (USC) was to enhance every organisation's policy practice from race relations to equal opportunities. The shared common aspiration on the agenda is the recruitment of ethnic minority employees. If we analyse the structure of the Committee in Figure 1 below, we will notice that it is not based on a hierarchical structure. Instead, the organisation is based on equality, appropriately in line with its theme of promoting racial equality and equal opportunities.

FIGURE 1
THE ORGANISATIONAL STRUCTURE OF THE SCOTTISH
UNIFORMED SERVICES' COMMITTEE

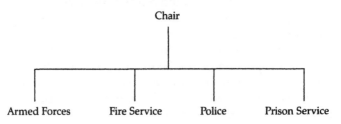

The position of *chair* operates on a rotation system, and every six months the position passes on to a representative from a different service. This ensures that no one service is dominant and the outcomes of meetings reflects the views of all representatives.

RECRUITMENT POTENTIAL OF THE DIFFERENT SERVICES

Obstacles to Recruitment

One of the main problems with the uniformed services in the UK has been with the internal culture of these organisations, a culture which has been resistant to change, and a culture which has consequently not been conducive to attracting ethnic minorities. As society has evolved and changed, the services have remained static. This unwillingness to change has meant that whilst society has become more cosmopolitan, the services have not recognised this change and have carried on as static rather than dynamic organisations, unwilling to accept that society is changing, and instead still holding on to the premise that change is not essential and that the current status quo is satisfactory. The services are becoming increasingly detached from society.[20] In many ways, the services rely on the support and even the help of communities to do their job. This bond must be re-established, otherwise the services will lose their credibility and will be unable to carry on their work effectively. This is a harsh lesson which the armed forces have embraced, all be it that they had no choice, and change was to an extent imposed upon them. The forces for a long time failed to acknowledge racism as a problem and did not even monitor statistics on recruits and as a result left themselves with a huge task to turn things around, which they appear now to be doing with some success. This example must be followed by the other services. It is important for any organisation to recognise the excellent skills of its employees and to praise them for it. This not only shows respect for the individual but also discloses to society that talents are recognised irrespective of class, creed or colour.

The potential to recruit ethnic minorities into the ranks of the uniformed services is hampered by the existence of barriers. These barriers can be divided into internal barriers such as racism, and the nature of the occupation, and those which are external such as education, and parental pressure, which are largely outside the control of the services. It is clear that the internal barriers are the ones which the services have some semblance of control over and can shape for example by creating conditions for racial accommodation and a better working environment. They have little or no control over the external ones. Some of these barriers are common to all of the services, while others are unique to a particular service. In addition these obstacles afflict the services on a national basis and are not unique to the Scottish services.

In the prison service, for example, the two main barriers are perceptions of racism and the nature of the job. In relation to the first, fear of racial discrimination at the hands of fellow officers and at the hands of white inmates has been well documented. In addition there has been the barrage of racism suffered by black and Asian prisoners at the hands of both white inmates and prison officers. In one major prison in Scotland, community organisations were involved in resolving up to 60 cases a year related to racial abuse and harassment.[21] Secondly, the nature of the job is testimony to the fact that many members of ethnic groups just could not envisage a career in an occupation viewed as 'rough and tough' and one which places high demands on an individual's physical and mental capacities. The threat to personal safety is high when dealing with dangerous inmates, and trying to break up jail riots and fights.

For the police, the three major stumbling blocks to minority recruitment, are negative perceptions of racism, experience of police in the country of origin of ethnic minority individuals, and failure to pass the entrance examination. Racism is an issue which has bedevilled the police and destroyed confidence among the community. As well as the Lawrence case and the subsequent Macpherson report, a *Guardian*/ICM poll[22] showed that 1 in 4 of the general public said that they believed that the police tend to be racist or were very racist, while 33% believed that the police did not treat black or Asian people fairly. Further lambasting for the police came from a report by Her Majesty's Inspectorate of Constabulary,[23] which said that almost every police force in Britain was failing in its duty to recruit and retain officers from ethnic minorities. Another reason cited was that minorities had negative perceptions of the police service in their country of origin. They had witnessed and in some cases, experienced brutality and corruption at the hands of the police. Inspector Findlay of Strathclyde Police suggests that: "forces in such countries try to rule, govern and police by force".[24] The truth is that developing countries are usually impoverished, therefore it is often possible to buy officers and other government employees. The situation is markedly different in the United Kingdom since "we are in a better financial position to pay our officers reasonably well".[25] Another argument often cited by officers is that ethnic minorities do express an interest in joining but fail the entrance examination. This is a charge which many race groups find surprising given that a large proportion of ethnic minorities tend to pursue education beyond school age and are subsequently educated to post-school level.

For the fire service, perceptions of racism and lack of awareness about a career in the service have been pivotal in the failure to attract ethnic minorities. Lack of awareness about job opportunities was stressed by Robert Deans, Station Officer at Strathclyde Fire Brigade.[26] It was noticeable that many ethnic minorities had little or no conception about the exact role played by the fire service. The point the Station Officer was trying to stress was that the fire service is not only concerned with fires but also transport accidents, industrial accidents, flooding, and explosions. Other duties subsumed assisting the police and ambulance service as well as rescuing animals. The fire service's racist tendencies were highlighted by an official report which condemned it "as a bastion of vicious sexism, persistent racism and wholesale homophobia".[27] In Scotland, scrutiny of the Scottish Fire Service has revealed the service's limited success in attracting ethnic minorities and it has been branded racist.[28] The fact is that the fire service does not have a problem recruiting from the indigenous population and is normally inundated with applications.

The armed services have faced a plethora of barriers to ethnic recruitment, and these barriers are still some way from being overcome. Perceptions of racism fuelled by media reporting has always been identified as a major impediment.

Zugbach and Ishaq have comprehensively charted the management of race relations in the armed forces and the recruitment of ethnic minorities into the services.[29] As with the fire service, lack of awareness about the armed services is suggested as being a factor. Indeed, a recent survey by the author of ethnic Muslims revealed that it was the top reason cited by interviewees (27%), as to why they felt that ethnic minorities were not joining the armed forces.[30] However, the services are attempting to address this, in particular the Royal Navy which runs a two-week 'personal development course'. The idea was to give individuals an opportunity to explore what life would be like in the navy. There has also been the establishment of the Ethnic Minority Recruitment Team, which makes regular visits to Scotland and its remit is "to visit various organisations throughout Glasgow to raise awareness of the opportunities available to young people thinking about pursuing a career in the armed forces".[31] This lack of awareness is also evident in the context of the forces' equal opportunities policy, with ethnic minorities not being aware that many of the perceived obstacles had now been addressed, for example, dietary, dress and religious needs.

There has been significant difficulty in convincing parents that the services offered a viable career prospect, and given the traditional strong family bonding among ethnic minority families, this is likely to influence the decision-making of potential recruits. Other serious barriers are that the forces have to compete with education which minority groups tend to pursue more vigorously than the indigenous population,[32] particularly those in the critical age-group, 17–22. Pakistani and Indian children in particular were inclined to stay on in further education till the age of 23. This makes it difficult to recruit ethnic minorities below the age of 23. Furthermore, minorities, like the indigenous population, tend to discriminate between the forces when deciding to make a choice. Evidence from officers interviewed show that the Army is more attractive than the RAF, which in turn is more preferable to the Royal Navy. This is shown in Tables 2 and 3 (opposite) which reveal that the number of enquiries and applications made to the armed services in Scotland were dominated by the Army.

Whilst a great deal of interest is shown in the forces at the enquiry stage this declines markedly in the actual number of applications being made. Tables 2 and 3 show that while there were 126 enquiries made to the services by ethnic minorities, only 65 of them took their enquiry a stage further and made an application to one of the services. This raises the question of whether those who are dealing with such enquiries are marketing the services effectively. How well informed are such individuals on racial issues? Can they explain in depth the equality issue and cultural sensitivity adopted by the services to young ethnic minorities? Can they accentuate to ethnic minorities the equal opportunities policy avidly fostered by the MoD?

TABLE 2
NUMBER OF ENQUIRIES MADE TO THE ARMED SERVICES IN SCOTLAND

Service	Year	Total All Groups	Total Ethnic Minorities
Royal Navy	1998/99	2,069	16
Army	1998/99	7,424	87
Royal Air Force	1998/99	3,437	23
Total	1998/99	12,930	126

Source: Defence Analytical Services Agency (DASA).

TABLE 3
NUMBER OF APPLICATIONS MADE TO THE ARMED SERVICES IN SCOTLAND

Service	Year	Total All Groups	Total Ethnic Minorities
Royal Navy	1998/99	1,483	9
Army	1998/99	4,242	41
Royal Air Force	1998/99	2,153	15
Total	1998/99	7,878	65

Source: Defence Analytical Services Agency (DASA).

Since Britain is a heterogeneous society, the need for ethnic minorities within the armed services is deemed to be important. The Army representative on the USC believes that "ethnic minorities are a part of the United Kingdom, the army has to reflect the ethnic groupings".[33] Squadron Leader Bob Bamford, the RAF representative, agrees that "colour and background should be insignificant as long as a person could do their job".[34]

The various barriers highlighted above show that despite the differing nature of the occupation offered by each of the services, some of the problems such as racism afflict all of them, therefore the criticism that the armed forces have often received that racism is attributable to the unique culture of the armed forces is unfair. It is more viable to argue that that racism is society's problem, which employees, who are recruited from that same society, reflect in the work they do for the services. Even more so than for the armed forces and the prison service, the police and fire services need to make tackling racism a top priority since they are in direct contact with the communities whom they endeavour to serve. It is surprising that the armed forces have long been singled out for some time for promoting a culture of racism. Surely, there is a case for the police and fire service, where the situation is no better, to be similarly coaxed.

In Table 4 below the barriers faced by each of the uniformed services is summarised.

TABLE 4
PRINCIPAL IMPEDIMENTS TO SERVICE RECRUITMENT

Service	Main Barriers
Armed Forces	Education; racism; parental pressure; and lack of awareness
Police	Racism; negative perceptions of police in country of origin; and entrance examination
Fire	Racism; and lack of awareness
Prison	Racism; and nature of occupation

It is also worth considering that those services which face a general recruitment problem such as the armed forces are perhaps in a better situation to recruit more minorities because they can adapt their existing recruitment measures to embrace all sections of society. In other words they already have a framework in place. In contrast, for those uniformed services such as the fire and police which do not face a widespread recruitment problem, it is more difficult because their incentive to pursue policies designed specifically to attract minorities is less. They would rather continue to recruit in the conventional fashion replacing those who leave voluntarily or retire with whoever wishes to join.

Current Service Performance and Initiatives to Increase Ethnic Minority Representation

This section assesses where the various services stand today and the strategies being used by the Scottish uniformed services to turn their recruitment potential into reality. There are certain yardsticks which can be used in order to determine the degree of progressiveness of an organisation's commitment to equal opportunities. In Table 5 below a ranking of 1 indicates that the relevant policy is in place. A ranking of 2 indicates that while the policy has been adopted it has not yet reached the stage of implementation. A ranking of 3 indicates that the organisation has realised the necessity for a particular policy and is considering it or it is in the process of consultation. A ranking of 4 suggests a definite weakness as the policy concerned is non-existent, and there are no plans currently for its inception.

TABLE 5
RANKING OF POLICY BY SERVICE

	Armed Forces	Fire	Police	Prison
Monitoring	1	3	1	4
Equal Opportunities Policy	1	1	1	1
Action Plans	1	2	1	2
Recruitment Targets	1	4	1	4
Grievance Procedures	1	1	1	1
Race Awareness Training	1	3	1	4

Table 5 shows that both the armed services and the police are well advanced in terms of having put in place a series of practices and policies, often viewed as synonymous with a credible commitment to equal opportunities and racial equality. Both the fire and prison services have much work to do, as neither of them currently monitor statistics on the personnel they recruit. The weakness of the fire and prison services in their commitment to equal opportunities is further apparent, as neither have set any feasible targets for ethnic minority recruitment, and currently do not have race awareness courses on the agenda of their employees' training.

The concept of ranking the services serves a beneficial function as it indicates where the services stand today, while, at the same time, highlighting areas which need to be enhanced and on which work needs to be done as a matter of necessity. However, as the author's works on the armed forces[35] have shown, even those services which are relatively advanced in adhering to equal opportunities and racial equality, are not immune from ethnic minority recruitment problems. The reason for this lies in the fact that as we have seen there are other factors which come into the equation when minorities consider a career in the uniformed services, and because the existence of policies does not mean that problems are immediately alleviated. Racism in an organisation does not cease to exist simply because an organisation embraces an equal opportunities policy.

Cole[36] emphasises that an important aspect of any equal opportunities policy is monitoring: "The employer needs to ascertain how many employees fall into the categories concerned and where they work, what jobs they do and what training and career development they might have received. This information can provide the basis for assessing where arbitrary discrimination may be occurring." When it comes to monitoring the armed forces are advanced in this process as are the police. Strathclyde Police, for example, monitors the number of ethnic minority police officers and special officers it employs. However, neither the Scottish fire service nor the prison service monitor statistics. The prison officer on the USC is only able to estimate that there are currently between 15 and 20 ethnic minority officers employed in the Scottish prison service.[37] It is startling that the prison headquarters do not keep such statistics. In an open admission during an interview, the prison officer heavily criticised the prison headquarters for not keeping statistics on the racial composition of its employees.[38] The Station Officer for the fire service said that he could estimate that there were probably only a handful of ethnic minorities working in the fire service.[39] Therefore, since in the fire and prison services the number of ethnic minorities employed was eminently small, these services were able to provide reasonably accurate estimates, even though statistics were not officially monitored. Monitoring is also important if recruitment targets have been set. After all, if statistics on personnel are not monitored then how can an organisation measure whether targets are being realised? So the fire and prison services are lagging behind the country as a whole.

When it comes to having an actual equal opportunities policy in the form of a written document as opposed to just claiming to be an equal opportunities employer, all four services are well advanced in this area, and are able to produce literature to back this up. For the armed services in Scotland, given that the British armed forces have in place a very comprehensive equal opportunities policy, it is merely a case of ensuring that the advances made nationally are applied effectively in Scotland so that there are no discrepancies in the level of performance and commitment at the regional level. According to the Army officer[40] on the USC the British Army's equal opportunity practices represent a powerful recruitment tool. That is why Equal Opportunity Advisers from all three armed services attend the Equal Opportunities Training Centre at the Royal Military College of Science, Shrivenham for a five-day course.[41] This is the only armed services equal opportunities course of its type in Europe.[42] However, despite all four services being able to produce an equal opportunities document, this in itself has not been sufficient to prevent problems from surfacing such as claims of racism. The reason for this is because the reality of the situation does not necessarily parallel the policies that have been devised. In order to do justice to equal opportunities the services have to strive to make sure that the policy is adhered to vehemently.

In order to see how committed the services are in wanting to recruit minorities, it is vital that recruitment targets are set. This may well help to demonstrate commitment, as failure to meet targets may be construed both inside and outside as an indication of organisational failure. While the Home Office has set national recruitment targets for the uniformed services, in Scotland only the armed services and the police have stipulated targets as part of their commitment. Strathclyde Police, the largest police force in Scotland, has specifically pledged to increase the number of ethnic minority officers from 0.2% to 0.5% within five years.[43]

Recruiting is all very well, but all the effort can be wasted unless appropriate and credible efforts are made to retain minorities once they are recruited. In particular, how do the uniformed services deal with grievances related to alleged racial discrimination, which may arise? Grievances which arise have to be dealt with because neglecting these can lead to conflict in the workplace and low morale, which in turn can have a detrimental effect on the standard of service delivered. All four services have procedures in place to deal with grievances and to take effective disciplinary action against those found guilty of racial harassment or of bullying. Such commitment is a vital part of establishing an organisation's commitment to equal opportunities in the workplace and sends out a positive message to ethnic minorities that they will not be neglected once recruited.

Additionally, another area worth exploring is the idea of making attendance at race awareness courses a requirement for all white recruits or those from the indigenous population. While attendance at race awareness courses need not be viewed as imperative for all organisations it can be useful for those organisations where there have been well-documented cases of racism. It just so happens that all of the services being looked at in this paper have had to confront accusations of racism. Both the armed services and the police have taken on board race awareness training, with all Scottish police forces running race awareness courses, as well as all of the armed services. Once again both the prison and fire services lag behind. The fire service has only recently considered it as an option, while for the prison service the idea of race awareness training has not even reached the stage of consideration. However, given the current climate and the debate on racism in the services it is difficult to see how long both these services can justify the absence of such a policy from their programme of action.

Finally, it is all good and well having an equal opportunities policy and even disseminating it but such policies are not always sufficient in inducing or convincing minorities to join. What are required are vigorous action plans, embodying a variety of strategies, namely continued input of time and resources. In this respect the situation is that all of the services in Scotland mirror the national situation by having action plans and all of them are making positive progress in this area. However the fire and prison services have only recently started to formulate their own initiatives. Thus far they have relied on joint initiatives which have been organised by the police and armed services. Below there is a more detailed look at the various methods that have been deployed by the services.

Action plans used to encourage recruitment of minorities

The notion of an action plan has a wide remit and the four uniformed services have all acknowledged the need to have such a plan. This is based on the realisation that the services will have to reach out to the ethnic minority community rather than wait for the minorities to make the first move. However, at present only the police and the armed forces have deployed a range of measures as part of their action plans to encourage recruitment of minorities. The fire and prison services are still in the infancy stages of developing strategies to put in place, and have till now only participated in measures which have been in conjunction with the police and the armed forces. So what have the services done to raise their profile to the ethnic minority community?

Liaison with ethnic minority community organisations has been a chief approach adopted by the services, as it represents an important element in the recruitment drive, and helps to facilitate the marketing strategy of the services. Home Secretary, Jack Straw, has emphasised that there should be "partnership and involvement with black and Asian people and their representative bodies".[44] The extensive work done in unison with community organisations highlights the fact that the Uniformed Services' Committee is keen to foster a partnership with the community. There are many facets to the way in which liaison with organisations assists the services. To begin with, the services seek the advice of community bodies in matters related to equal opportunities and race relations, in order to ensure that they are clear about the legal side of things. Advice is also pursued in relation to developing an effective equal opportunities regime, with the services seeking clarification on cultural and religious aspects such as dietary requirements, dress code and language.

More recently ethnic minority organisations have provided support to arrange events such as recruitment fairs, ethnic minority festivals, and sports galas where the services aimed at having a high profile presence.[45] Such events are ideal because they attract minorities from the desired recruiting age-group and thus represent fertile ground for strengthening ethnic minority recruitment. These events also served an additional purpose as they provided a great opportunity for the uniformed services to familiarise themselves with the different ethnic communities and allow a process of gradual integration to take shape. During its first year the Uniformed Services' Committee has organised a number of events with the specific aim of attracting ethnic minority recruits. One of the events organised was a Uniformed Services' Seminar on 17 March 1999. It was "a co-ordinated recruitment seminar, the first in Britain, which brought together senior figures from the armed forces, police, fire and prison services".[46]

Extensive advertising has been a very important ingredient in the recruitment drive. The plan of action in this area has centred on the dissemination of literature and media exposure. Service representatives have also participated in community radio shows. However, television has only been exploited by the armed forces. The other uniformed services have still not gone down this path. Evidence from a survey of Muslim perceptions[47] revealed that television was the medium by which 55% of interviewees had seen adverts by the armed services. This is a clear indication that television represents a fruitful outlet that can be exploited. Advertising is an expensive venture, so it is imperative that it is successfully designed.

While visits have also been made to religious places, this is a tactic which may reap less fruition. Recent evidence has shown that places of worship are viewed strictly for that purpose and ethnic minority youth do not tend to notice literature at these places.[48]

Education has also played a role in the recruitment picture. Courses at educational establishments have been devised to help minorities who are having difficulty with entrance tests.[49] This is particularly important in the case of the police who have claimed for some time that ethnic minority recruitment was being hampered by the failure of individuals to pass the entrance exam. Moreover, representatives from the services have visited a number of schools in Central Scotland, where there is a high concentration of ethnic minorities, to publicise career opportunities in the services.

A method which has been pioneered by the services and used for some time by both the police and the fire service is the use of volunteers who wish to assist the services. For instance in the police there are special constables, who are normally unpaid and wish to aid the police and the community.[50] The fire service also employs volunteers.[51] Such voluntary posts are an ideal way of allowing volunteers to get a feel of what it would be like to work in a uniformed service through practical experience. Both the police and the fire services currently have ethnic minority volunteers in their ranks.

If the uniformed services are to be successful in their ethnic minority recruitment drives, they must capitalise on the fact that in April 1999 there were over 24,000 vacancies available across the uniformed services. From Table 6 (p.132) it can be seen that the British Army, the largest of the armed services, has more jobs to offer than the Royal Navy and Royal Air Force. Strathclyde Police, the Scottish Prison Service and Strathclyde Fire Brigade have fewer jobs to offer than the armed services because they are comparatively smaller organisations. It is inevitable that in a capitalist economy, unemployment will always persist, and statistics show that in relative terms ethnic minorities are predominantly the most suffering group in British society. The unemployment figures in 1995/96 for white people were 11%, while for ethnic minorities they were 18%.[52] Therefore there is a pool of human resources to be targeted.

SUMMARY

So what has this chapter disclosed? It has illustrated that working in partnership has been an effective method of enticing four Scottish uniformed services to play a leading

TABLE 6
NUMBER OF VACANCIES OFFERED BY THE UNIFORMED
SERVICES IN SCOTLAND

Uniformed Services	No. of Posts Offered
Strathclyde Police*	400
Scottish Prison Service	250
Royal Navy	4,700
British Army	15,000
Royal Air Force	4,000
Strathclyde Fire Brigade*	60–80

*In the case of both the police and fire service, figures were only available for the Strathclyde region.

Source: Uniformed Services' Seminar, Glasgow, 1999.

role in overcoming barriers that prevent ethnic minorities from joining the uniformed services in Scotland. The uniformed services have forged a unique alliance, in the form of the Uniformed Services' Committee, which is collectively trying to recruit ethnic minorities into the services.

The predicament facing the Scottish uniformed services mirrors the national picture, with current ethnic minority representation in the services being well below the proportion of minorities represented in the population. All the services face impediments in their bid to address this low representation, with the most common obstacle being racism, which is applicable to all the services. In view of this it is fair to argue that a well-advanced commitment to equal opportunities, which is credible and convincing would be a worthy goal.

This chapter has also shown that the armed services and the police, the two services which have perhaps been at the centre of most attention in recent years are also coincidentally the most advanced, both regionally, and in the case of the armed services, nationally. Both these services have in place recruitment targets, which drive their desire to fulfil their objectives, monitoring of statistics on personnel composition as a measurement of whether targets set are being met, and race awareness courses as part of their employees' training.

However, while the prison and fire services have still much to do, the chances of them attaining a level which is on par with the armed forces and the police is more realistic if the Uniformed Services' Committee can maintain the status of a permanent forum. Indeed despite lagging behind the police and armed forces, the prison and fire services have since the formation of the committee made progress. The fire service has started consultations on putting into place a policy on monitoring the number of ethnic minorities in the service, and the prison service has also began to show more interest in addressing its weaknesses. Prior to the setting up of the committee neither service took the race issue very seriously. At present the main weaknesses in the fire and prison services' commitment to equal opportunities, which it is hoped that they will address under the auspices of the committee, is that neither service monitors statistics on ethnic minority recruits, neither have set recruitment targets for minority recruitment and neither has race awareness courses as part of their employees' training.

Since the establishment of the Uniformed Services Committee in early 1999, some of the services have taken on board new ideas and methods for recruiting, which supplemented existing ones. Liaison with ethnic minority organisations who have provided them with advice and direction, extensive advertising, interaction with the community via sports galas, recruitment fairs have all been embraced by the services. This has also permitted the public to acknowledge the existence of the services. These plans of action continue to be nurtured.

The job of the services in Scotland is made harder by the fact that there are far fewer ethnic minorities residing in Scotland in comparison to England. Secondly, since most minorities reside in the central belt covering major cities such as Glasgow and Edinburgh, efficient use of resources demands that much of the work and methods deployed be confined to this region, therefore other regions of Scotland tend to get left out, and while there are only sporadic pockets of minorities in for example Aberdeen, they can largely be oblivious to the message being portrayed by the services. The

Uniformed Services' Committee is admittedly still in its infancy stage. It will naturally take time before it is able to establish the long-term effectiveness of the uniformed services in boosting ethnic minority recruitment. While the work described in this chapter is based on Scotland, there is no reason why a policy approach similar to the Uniformed Services' Committee analysed here cannot be applied on a national level. It would be profitable for other councils in different regions of the UK as a whole to foster the same uniformed services' forum. There is also no reason why such a committee should only incorporate the four uniformed services. There are many other public sector services such as Royal Mail and the probation service, which should seek participation, and who should be encouraged. The tax reliant public sector organisations should set the standards for the private sector to follow. It also worth bearing in mind that the attention and publicity being assigned to the uniformed services in this paper is in no way an attempt to show that these services are out on their own. There are other professions which also need to address the question of ethnic minority recruitment. These include the legal profession, the health service and the civil service.[53] These organisations need to implement measures and comply with equal opportunities as precedence rather than imposed pressure from the Commission for Racial Equality and criticism from the media. In the current political climate, no public sector institution can expect to escape from both its moral and legal obligation to provide equality of opportunity at the workplace.

NOTES

1. Home Office. *Race Equality – The Home Secretary's Employment Targets*, July 1999.
2. *BBC Ceefax Service*, 29 July 1999.
3. The following is a selection of some of the works: Simon Holdaway: "Ethnic Minority Recruitment into the Police: A Summary of Research Findings", mimeo, 1990; Michael King *et al.*, "Ethnic Minorities and Recruitment to the Solicitor's Profession", Brunel University, 1990; James Sheffield and Asifa Hussain, "Organisational Barriers and Ethnicity in the Scottish NHS", *Management in Medicine*, Vol.13, Nos. 4 and 5, 1999, pp. 263–84.
4. A. W. Bradley, "Racial Discrimination in the Public Sector", *Public Law*, Autumn 1991, pp. 317–25.

5. N. Fielding, "Policing's Dark Secret: The Career Paths of Ethnic Minority Officers", *Sociological Research Online*, Vol.4, No.1, pp. u38–u48, 1999.
6. S. Beishon, Virdee, S.. and Hagell, A., *Nursing in a Multi-Ethnic NHS*, Policy Studies Institute, HMSO n.d.
7. James Sheffield and Asifa Hussain, "Organisational Barriers and Ethnicity in the Scottish NHS", *Management in Medicine*, Vol.13, Nos. 4 and 5, 1999, pp. 263–84.
8. Diane Abbott, "Racism is Real", *Nursing Standard*, Vol.11, No.17, 1997.
9. Sonia Liff and Linda Dickens, "Ethics and Equality: Reconciling False Dilemmas" in *Ethical Issues in Contemporary Human Resource Management*, Marshall and Winstanley (eds). London: Macmillan, 1999.
10. See *Daily Telegraph*, 6 December 1998 and for more information on the Lawrence Inquiry see *Stephen Lawrence Inquiry: report of an inquiry by Sir William Macpherson*, Public Stationery Office, 1999.
11. Ibid.
12. Ibid.
13. Office for Public Management, *Review of Ethnic Minority Initiatives: Final Report*, 1996, London: OPM.
14. *The Times*, 30 January 1997.
15. *The Times*, 21 March 1997.
16. *The Times*, 25 March 1998.
17. *Daily Telegraph*, 25 February 1999.
18. Ibid. 22 February 1999.
19. Home Office. Race Equality – The Home Secretary's Employment Targets, July 1999.
20. This perceived detachment has been well documented in the case of the armed services. See Antony Beevor: "The Army and Modern Society" in Hew Strachan (ed.) *The British Army, Manpower and Society into the Twenty-First Century*, London: Frank Cass Publishers, 2000.
21. Interviewee Edward Davidson, Prison Liaison Officer for the Scottish Prison Service referring to Barlinnie Prison in Glasgow.
22. *Guardian*, 9 February 1999.
23. *Her Majesty's Chief Inspector of Constabulary Annual Report 1998–99*, Stationery Office, 1999.
24. Interview with Inspector Iain Findlay, Strathclyde Police, April 1999.
25. Ibid.
26. Interview with Robert Deans, Station Officer, Strathclyde Fire Brigade, July 1999.
27. *Fire Services for Scotland Annual Report 1998–99*, Stationery Office, 1999.
28. This was stressed in the *Fire Services for Scotland Annual Report 1998–99*, Stationery Office, 1999.
29. Reggie von Zugbach and Mohammed Ishaq, "Managing Race Relations in the British Army", forthcoming in *Defence Analysis*, June 2000.
30. Asifa Hussain and Mohammed Ishaq, "British Muslims' Perceptions of the Armed Forces", forthcoming.
31. *Scotland's Oracle*, 10 March 1999.
32. Leslie *et al.*, "Staying on in Full-time Education: Reasons for Higher Participation Rates among Ethnic Minority Males and Females", *Economica*, Vol.66, No.261, 1999, pp. 63–77.
33. Interview with Lieutenant Colonel David Steele, British Army, May 1999.
34. Interview with Squadron Leader, Bob Bamford, Royal Air Force, May 1999.
35. Ishaq, Zugbach and Hussain, "Ethnic Minority Recruitment and Retention in the British Army", forthcoming.
36. See Gerald Cole, *Personnel Management*, Letts Educational, London, 1997.
37. Interview with Edward Davidson, Prison Liaison Officer, Scottish Prison

Service, June 1999.
38. Ibid.
39. Interview with Robert Deans, Station Officer, Strathclyde Fire Brigade, July 1999.
40. Interview with Lieutenant Colonel David Steele, British Army, May 1999.
41. Details of this are contained in: *Ministry of Defence/Commission for Racial Equality Action Plan Annual Report, 1998–1999*.
42. Ibid.
43. These targets were specified in Strathclyde Police's strategic action plan, details of which can be found in *Her Majesty's Chief Inspector of Constabulary for Scotland Annual Report 1998–99*, Stationery Office, 1999.
44. *Race Equality – The Home Secretary's Employment Targets*, July 1999, Home Office.
45. A number of events were held across Scotland in 1998 and 1999. These attracted media attention.
46. *The Times*, 18 March 1999.
47. Asifa Hussain and Mohammed Ishaq, "British Muslims' Perceptions of the Armed Forces", forthcoming, 2000.
48. Ibid.
49. One such course is run by James Watt College in Glasgow on a full-time basis.
50. Interview with Iain Findlay, Police Inspector, Strathclyde Police, April 1999.
51. Interview with Robert Deans, Station Officer, Strathclyde Fire Brigade, July 1999.
52. See Commission for Racial Equality fact-sheet, *Employment and Unemployment;* and *Labour Force Survey*, Summer 1995–Spring 1996.
53. Statistics show that ethnic minority representation in civil service departments, the legal profession and the NHS is low and there are barriers placed in the path of promotion. For example there are no ethnic minorities among the 98 High Court judges and in the health service ethnic minority doctors were consistently overlooked when it came to promotion.

8

The Times are a' Changin':
Homosexuality and the Armed Forces

ALEX ALEXANDROU
Cranfield University, Royal Military College of Science

INTRODUCTION

The times are certainly a' changin' for the British military regarding the issue of homosexuals being allowed to serve in the Armed Forces. Homosexuality in military organisations is not a new phenomenon, it has existed since Ancient Greek and Roman times, where it was not only tolerated but also encouraged, whilst two of Britain's most celebrated war poets of the First World War, Siegfried Sassoon and Wifred Owen were both homosexuals who hid their true orientation.

As the twentieth century ended and the new millennium dawned, the issue of the British Armed Forces openly allowing homosexuals to serve has continued to vex military and political institutions alike. However, attitudes have already been changing, particularly amongst the North American, European and Antipodean nations. This has been partly in response to changes in social attitudes and partly in response to legal actions and judgements. Nevertheless, Britain has for some time been out of step with other countries with regard to this question.

The principal aim of this chapter is to examine how the present Government and military institutions of the United Kingdom have had to address this issue in the past year. It is not the intention of this chapter or Chapter 9 to enter into the moral debate on this issue. This has been addressed in great depth by a number of commentators, notably Armitage,[1] Dandeker and Paton,[2] Deakin,[3] Frost,[4] Lustig-Prean[5] and Natzio.[6]

Whilst homosexuality has become far more widely accepted in society, this has not been the case within military circles, and pressures for change are causing great consternation. It is fair to state that Armed Forces are now being faced with three choices; to maintain a ban on homosexuals, instigate a policy of not asking personnel what their sexual orientation is, or openly recruiting homosexuals.

As a precursor to examining how the United Kingdom has dealt with this sensitive issue, I will briefly outline how a number of nations have dealt with the open admission of homosexuals into their military organisations.

FOREIGN MILITARY ORGANISATIONS AND THEIR RESPONSE TO ADMITTING HOMOSEXUALS

In many Armed Forces, homosexuals are still barred from serving but as the gay campaigning group Stonewall's[7] research shows, a significant number do not discriminate on the basis of sexual orientation. These include: Australia, Austria, Belgium, Canada, Denmark, France, Greece, Ireland, Israel, Netherlands, New Zealand, Norway, Spain, South Africa, Sweden and Switzerland.

A number of examples from the above mentioned nations will now be examined to show how and why they have adopted policies that do not bar entry into their Armed Services based on sexual orientation.

Sweden

Kier,[8] describes how in 1987, Sweden prohibited discrimination on the basis of sexual orientation in the military. The majority of Swedish military and political officials supported this initiative. The new policy has resulted in few, if any, problems and despite the lack of hard evidence, the Swedes report that the participation of homosexuals has not hurt unit readiness, effectiveness, cohesion or morale.

Australia

In 1992, following a review of procedures, the Department of Defence announced that sexual orientation would no longer be a bar to serving in the Services. This was formalised in 1994 when the Australian Defence Force implemented a policy based on unacceptable behaviour irrespective of sexual orientation and this is enshrined in a code of conduct,[9] which accepted the principle that sexual relations are part of adult life and are a private matter. This policy was updated in 1999.[10] It can be described as a neutral policy and one it seems on which the British authorities have modelled their own code of conduct quite closely.

Canada

According to Park[11] the situation in Canada was almost the opposite of the Swedish experience. She points out that the Canadian military were actively opposed to the lifting of the ban on homosexuals serving in the Armed Forces. However, in 1992, the Canadian courts ruled that the military had to remove all restrictions based on sexual orientation. To date, there is no evidence to suggest that this reversal of policy has been detrimental to the efficiency and effectiveness of the Canadian Armed Forces.

Israel

Gal[12] describes how in practice homosexuals had been integrated into the Israeli Defence Forces (IDF) since 1948, but it was not until 1993 that the IDF adopted a policy that did not discriminate on the basis of sexual orientation with regard to recruitment, assignments and promotion. IDF officials argue that homosexuals have caused few problems, have performed as well as anyone else and did not hinder readiness, effectiveness, cohesion or morale.

USA

During the 1992 American presidential campaign, Bill Clinton pledged to lift the ban on homosexuals serving in the United States Armed Services. However, as Kier,[13] clearly shows, once installed in the Oval office, he was unable to deliver on this pledge. The President encountered significant resistance from not only senior officers in the military, but also their supporters in Congress. By the summer of 1993, he had to admit defeat, but a compromise was reached. Congress passed a policy that allowed homosexuals to serve in the Services, as long as they did not reveal their sexual orientation. This is commonly described as the "Don't Ask, Don't Tell, Don't Pursue" policy. Little evidence has emerged to date to enable commentators to ascertain whether this policy is working and whether it is worth pursuing.

South Africa

This is an interesting example as the rights to personal privacy and freedom from discrimination are enshrined in Chapter 2 of the country's Constitution.[14] All public sector organisations, including the South African Defence Force (SADF), have to ensure that these rights are not transgressed by developing their human resource management and equal opportunities policies in line with the Constitution. The policy in respect to sexual orientation has been in place since 1998 in the SADF and it is too early to gauge the success or otherwise of this initiative.

HOMOSEXUALITY AND THE BRITISH ARMED FORCES

Background

Until January 2000, homosexuals were barred from serving in the Armed Forces by military law in the form of the Army Act 1955,[15] Air Force Act 1955[16] and the Naval Discipline Act 1955.[17] The Services also had immunity under the Sexual Offences Act 1967[18] but this was repealed by the Criminal Justice and Public Order Act 1994[19] which stated that military personnel could not be prosecuted under military law for homosexual acts that were not criminal in civilian law. However, members of the Armed Forces could still be dismissed and entry barred to homosexuals based on the administrative procedures of the three military acts and the MoD's guidelines on homosexuality.[20] This was the legal situation until a judgement by the European Court of Human Rights in September 1999[21] turned this whole issue on its head. The events leading up to and the reasons for this judgement will be briefly discussed in the next section.

From Rank Outsiders to Acceptable Insiders?

In 1991, an organisation called Rank Outsiders[22] was formed to provide confidential welfare, support, counselling and legal advice to serving and ex-serving lesbian and gay service personnel of all ranks. Its primary objective was to campaign for the admission of homosexuals into the Services. This pressure group succeeded in not only re-opening the debate of open homosexuality in the British Armed Forces, but also helping a number of ex-military gay personnel take cases through both the British courts and the European Court of Human Rights (ECHR)[23] in order to overturn the ban.

The personnel involved in the ECHR case were Duncan Lustig-Prean (former Royal Naval Lieutenant Commander), John Beckett (former Royal Navy Rating), Jeanette Smith (former Royal Air Force Nurse) and Graeme Grady (former Royal Air Force Sergeant). The four individuals had each been the subject of an investigation concerning their homosexuality, all had admitted their sexual orientation and each had been administratively discharged on the sole ground of their sexual orientation, in accordance with MoD policy. They were discharged in January 1995, July 1993, November 1994 and December 1994 respectively.[24]

In November 1995 the British Court of Appeal rejected their judicial review applications, which led to the four to lodge their applications with the ECHR on the 23 April, 11 July, 9 September and 6 September respectively. On 1 November 1998 in accordance with the European Convention on Human Rights, the cases were transmitted to the Court. On the 23 February 1999, the Court joined Mr Lustig-Prean and Mr Beckett's applications and Ms Smith's and Mr Grady's applications. On the same day the Court declared that their complaints were admissible and the cases were heard on the 18 May 1999.[25]

Lustig-Prean and Beckett complained that the investigations into their sexual orientation which led to the subsequent discharge from the Royal Navy, violated their right to respect for their private lives and that they had been discriminated against in contravention of Articles 8 and 14 respectively of the Convention.[26] Smith and Grady made the same complaints and they further complained that the MoD policy pertaining to homosexuals and consequent investigations and discharges were degrading and contrary to Article 3 of the Convention (which prohibits inhuman or degrading treatment or punishment). They also argued that the policy limited their right to express their sexual identity in violation of Article 10 that relates to freedom of expression and that they did not have effective domestic remedy for their complaints as required by Article 13.[27]

On 27 September 1999 the ECHR delivered the judgement that would have far reaching implications for the British Government and Armed Forces. In the case concerning Lustig-Prean and Beckett, the Court held that there had been a violation of Article 8 (the right to respect for private and family life) of the Convention. With regard to the Smith and Grady case it found that not only had Article 8 been violated but also Article 13, which relates to the right to an effective remedy. The Court reserved for separate judgements the issue of awards of just satisfaction under Article 41.[28]

Following the judgement the Secretary of State for Defence, George Robertson issued a statement[29] that accepted the ruling, indicating that its implications would be carefully considered and that recommendations would be made in due course. He also stated that other such cases in the MoD system would be put on hold.

Following a review of the judgement, George Robertson's successor, Geoffrey Hoon announced that the current ban on homosexuals serving in the Armed Forces was to be lifted with immediate effect.[30] He also stated that in light of the Court's decisions it was clear that the Ministry's existing policy was not legally sustainable and that a new one had to be introduced. He pointed out that a revised policy had been developed to ensure that it preserved the Services' operational effectiveness, respected the rights of the individual and took full account of the ECHR ruling and that the Chiefs of Staff were fully committed to it. The review had drawn on the experience of other countries, notably Australia, and a code of conduct with a service test had been drawn up to apply across the Forces, irrespective of service, rank, gender or sexual orientation.

Hoon went on to state that the aim of the code was to provide a clear framework within which service personnel could live and work and also which would complement existing policies on such issues as harassment, discrimination and bullying. He argued that the code was not an abstract legal document full of rules and regulations but was one that had been developed by experts from within the Services who understood the operational needs and day-to-day practicalities of the Forces. He pointed out that Commanding Officers had been issued with briefing packs to explain the code of conduct to those in their charge.[31]

CODE OF CONDUCT FOR ARMED FORCES PERSONNEL

This section will briefly outline the Code,[32] which has been split into the three distinct parts that cover the guiding principles, operational imperatives and the service test against which the Code can be considered.

Guiding Principles

• Sexual orientation is a private matter for the individual.

• Knowledge of an individual's sexual orientation is not a basis for discrimination.

• Incidents which involve the possible commission of civil or military offences, or which come to a Commanding Officer's attention through a formal complaint, should be investigated and dealt with in accordance with Service disciplinary or administrative procedures.

• The Service Test contained in the Code of Social Conduct should be applied when there is any doubt about the impact on operational effectiveness of any particular incident.

• The Armed Forces value the unique contribution which every individual makes to operational effectiveness, regardless of their sexual orientation.

• The Armed Forces respect the right to individual privacy of every Serviceman and woman and will only intervene in the private lives of individuals where it is necessary in the interests of preserving operational effectiveness.

• The new policy makes no moral judgements about an individual's sexual orientation.

• There is no place in the Armed Forces for harassment, bullying or victimisation.

- Commanders have a duty of care towards all those under their command.

Operational Imperatives

The code makes it quite clear that in the area of personal relationships, the overriding operational imperatives are to sustain team cohesion and to maintain trust and loyalty between commanders and those in their charge. It goes on to underline the fact that the standards of social behaviour within the Services need to be more demanding than those required by society at large.

The Service Test

The Code has a test against which Commanding Officers must consider possible cases of social misconduct. The Service Test asks the following question:

> "Have the actions or behaviour of an individual adversely impacted or are likely to impact on the efficiency or operational effectiveness of the Service?"

The code states that Commanding Officers will consider a series of key criteria that will establish the seriousness of the misconduct and its impact on operational effectiveness. In turn this will allow them to dispense the appropriate and proportionate level of sanction.

It is interesting to note that this policy has already been incorporated into the MoD's Armed Forces Overarching Personnel Strategy (AFOPS)[33] and the Army's Values and Standards policy.[34] The Code and the ECHR judgement will be discussed in greater detail in the next chapter.

THE FUTURE

The introduction of the Code and adherence to the ECHR judgement may not be enough if the prevailing view of the legal fraternity is to be accepted. A briefing note produced by Pinsent Curtis[35] points out that at present neither British domestic law nor European Community law prohibits discrimination based on sexual orientation though there have been strenuous calls for such behaviour to be outlawed. It points out that to date the Government has not committed itself to legislation, although it has announced that it will introduce a non-statutory code of practice in due course.

However, the Pinsent Curtis brief shows[36] that, in the event, the Government may well be overtaken by two recent developments. Firstly, at European level, the EU Commissioner for Employment and Social Affairs (Anna Diamantopoulou) has announced her intention to propose a Directive, which would, amongst other things, outlaw workplace discrimination against homosexuals. This is because the Treaty of Rome[37] did not authorise legislation in this area but the position has been changed by the Treaty of Amsterdam,[38] which came into force in the UK in January 2000. Secondly, the European Convention on Human Rights[39] as highlighted by the Lustig-Prean and Beckett and Smith and Grady cases and resultant judgements,[40] will form part of British law in the Human Rights Act[41] (that incorporates the Convention), which comes into force on 2 October 2000. The Act requires all public authorities including the Armed Forces to comply with the Convention. If they discriminate against an employee on grounds of sexual orientation, it is likely that they will be in breach of the Convention and liable to be sued in the British courts by the individual concerned.[42] This highlights an issue raised by Dandeker and Paton[43] who, when discussing the lifting on the ban on homosexuals serving in the Forces, pointed out that:

"... in the longer term, to command consensus within the armed services, serious practical issues would remain: would the armed services permit gay couples to dance at service events? What 'rights' in terms of accommodation and other benefits would accrue to such couples? And so on. In effect, can the military accede to demands for the normalisation of homosexual and heterosexual relationships before wider society has done so. The difficulty here is that 'gay political activists' are intent on focusing on the military precisely as a vehicle of that process of normalisation."

Lustig-Prean[44] may disagree with the final point but the issues raised by Dandeker and Paton are valid and will be put to the test not only by the Code but also by the Human Rights Act. They may well have long term implications for the Armed Forces in terms of the diversity and equality policies adopted and the reaction of heterosexual personnel, which in turn may affect the recently introduced AFOPS. Only time will tell.

NOTES

1. Michael Armitage, "Gay Warriors – Implications for Military Cohesion", in Gerald Frost (ed.), *Not Fit to Fight – The Cultural Subversion of the Armed Forces in Britain and America*, The Social Affairs Unit, London 1998, pp. 39–46.
2. Christopher Dandeker and Fiona Paton, *The Military and Social Change: A Personnel Strategy for the British Armed Forces*, The Centre For Defence Studies, Brassey's, London: 1997.
3. Stephen Deakin, "The British Army and Homosexuality", in Hew Strachan (ed.), *The British Army – Manpower and Society into the Twenty-First Century*, Frank Cass, London 2000, pp. 119–38.
4. Gerald Frost, "The Folly of Imposing a Liberal Vision on a Necessarily Illiberal Society", *RUSI Journal*, Vol. 144, No. 3, June 1999, pp. 93–6.
5. Duncan Lustig-Prean, "People are Discharged for one Private Aspect of their Private Lives, not for any Misconduct", *RUSI Journal*, Vol. 144, No. 3, June 1999, pp. 90–92.
6. Georgina Natzio, "Homosexuality – Can the Armed services Survive it?", *RUSI Journal*, Vol. 140, No. 6, December 1995, pp. 39–46.
7. Stonewall, "Memorandum of Evidence on the Ban on Lesbians and Gay Men in the Armed Forces" in the *Special Report from the Select Committee on the Armed Forces Bill*, Defence Select Committee, Session 1995–1996, HC 143, HMSO, London: 30 April 1996, pp. 178–1.
8. Elizabeth Kier, "Homosexuals in the U.S. Military – Open Integration and Combat Effectiveness", *International Security*, Vol.23, No.2, Fall 1998, pp. 5–39.
9. Department of Defence, *Unacceptable Sexual Behaviour by Members of the Australian Defence Force*, DI (G) PERS 35-3, DoD, Canberra: November 1994.
10. Department of Defence, *Discrimination, Harassment, Sexual Offences, Fraternisation and other Unacceptable Behaviour in the Australian Defence Force*, DI (G) PERS 35-3, DoD, Canberra March 1999.
11. Rosemary Park, "Opening the Canadian Forces to Gays and Lesbians", in *Gays and Lesbians in the Military*, Wilbur Scott and Sandra Stanley (eds.), Aldine de Gruyter, New York 1994, pp. 165–80.
12. Reuven Gal, "Gays in the Military: Policy and Practice in the Israeli Defence Forces", in *Gays and Lesbians in the Military*, Wilbur Scott and Sandra Stanley (Eds), Aldine de Gruyter, New York 1994, pp. 186–8.
13. Elizabeth Kier, op. cit.
14. *The Constitution of the Republic of South Africa, 1996*, (Act 108 of 1996), RSA, Pretoria.
15. *Army Act 1955*, HMSO, London.
16. *Air Force Act 1955*, HMSO, London.
17. *Naval Discipline Act 1955*, HMSO, London.
18. *Sexual Offences Act 1967*, HMSO, London.
19. *Criminal Justice and Public Order Act 1994*, HMSO, London.
20. Ministry of Defence, *Armed Forces Policy and Guidelines on Homosexuality*, MoD, London 1994.

21. European Court of Human Rights, *Judgements in the Cases of Lustig-Prean and Beckett v The United Kingdom and Smith and Grady v The United Kingdom*, ECHR, Strasbourg, 27 September 1999.
22. Rank Outsiders, "Memorandum of Evidence on Lesbian and Gay Service Personnel", in the *Special Report from the Select Committee on the Armed Forces Bill*, Defence Select Committee, Session 1995–1996, HC 143, HMSO, London: 30 April 1996, pp. 191–209.
23. European Court of Human Rights, op. cit.
24. Ibid.
25. Ibid.
26. Ibid.
27. Ibid.
28. Ibid.
29. Ministry of Defence, *Homosexuality and the Armed forces – European Court of Human Rights Judgement*, Press Release, 27 September 1999.
30. Geoffrey Hoon, Armed Forces (ECHR), *Hansard*, TSO, London: 12 January 2000, Columns 285–7.
31. Ibid.
32. Ministry of Defence, *Code of Conduct for Armed Forces Personnel*, MoD, London: 12 January 2000.
33. Ministry of Defence, *Armed Forces Overarching Personnel Strategy* ,MoD, London: February 2000.
34. British Army, *Values and Standards of the British Army*, AC No 63813, March 2000.
35. Pinsent Curtis, *Employment Law Bulletin, Discrimination on Grounds of Sexual Orientation – Latest Developments*, Pinsent Curtis, London: January 2000.
36. Ibid.
37. European Economic Community, *Treaty establishing the European Economic Community – Treaty of Rome*, EEC, Strasbourg: 1955.
38. European Community, *Treaty on European Union – Treaty of Amsterdam*, EC, Strasbourg: 1997.
39. *European Convention of Human Rights and Fundamental Freedoms*, Rome: 4 November 1950.
40. European Court of Human Rights, op. cit.
41. *Human Rights Act, 1998*, TSO, London.
42. Pinsent Curtis, op. cit.
43. Christopher Dandeker and Fiona Paton, op. cit, p. 75.
44. Duncan Lustig-Prean, op. cit.

147

9

Homosexuality and the Armed Forces: The Legal Position!

ALLAN ROSS

Cranfield University, Royal Military College of Science

INTRODUCTION

The recent *Lustig-Prean*[1] judgement of the European Court of Human Rights (hereafter the Court) had the potential to see the introduction of a new paradigm in human resource management for the armed forces. The findings of the Court required the Government and senior military staff to undertake a radical re-think of policy regarding homosexuality in the armed forces. This culminated in the announcement by the Defence Secretary that he had "asked the Chief of the Defence Staff to set in hand an urgent review of policy in that area".[2] The outcome of this has been the lifting of the ban on homosexuals serving in the armed forces and the imposition of a new 'Code of Conduct' (hereafter the Code) governing personal relationships in the armed forces, a Code that will cover all personal relationships not just homosexual relationships.

The Code is summarised in what the Government has termed 'The Service Test'. This simply asks the question:

> "Have the actions or behaviour of an individual adversely impacted or are they likely to impact on the efficiency or operational effectiveness of the Service?"[3]

The scope of this statement is reflected in the variety of examples of conduct the Government cites as being likely to fall within the remit of the Code. These include, but are not limited to:

> "unwelcome sexual attention in the form of physical or verbal conduct; over-familiarity with the spouses or partners of other Service personnel; displays of affection

which might cause offence to others; behaviour which damages or hazards the marriage or personal relationships of Service personnel or civilian colleagues within the wider defence community; and taking sexual advantage of subordinates."[4]

The armed forces are now faced with a Code of conduct which rather than ensuring equal treatment regardless of sexual orientation, acts more as a 'catch-all' allowing local commanders a wide ranging discretion in deciding what conduct is to be regarded as having or likely to have an "impact on the efficiency or operational effectiveness of the Service".[5] Whilst it is legitimate to argue that the need for a high standard of social behaviour is of greater importance within the armed forces than in society in general, it is questionable whether the removal of one highly specific and discriminatory ban followed by the imposition of a non-specific and highly subjective prohibition is the right way forward. This is especially the case in light of the fact that within the term 'personal relationships' homosexuality is likely to be regarded by many local commanders as being the most significant factor to 'impact on the efficiency or operational effectiveness of the Service'. The imposition of the Code also raises the issue of why such a Code is required in the first place. If it has never been deemed necessary to govern heterosexual relationships by reference to such a code, and if the removal of the ban on serving homosexuals was needed in order to satisfy the requirement of non-discrimination, as laid down by the Court in its case law, would it not have been a less problematic solution to include all personal relationships under the previous non-codified system. Certainly the Minister appears to have ignored the advice of the armed forces experts on homosexuality in the services, the Homosexuality Policy Assessment Team (HPAT), and the advice that they gave in February 1996.

"Alternative options were considered by the HPAT including a code of conduct applicable to all, a policy based on the individual qualities of homosexual personnel, lifting the ban and relying on service personnel reticence, the "don't ask, don't tell" solution offered by the USA and a "no open homosexuality" code. *It concluded that no policy alternative could be identified which avoided risks for fighting power with the same certainty as the present policy* and which, in consequence, would not be strongly opposed by the service population".[6] (Emphasis added)

With the HPAT having rejected a number of proposed policies, including the Code, it remains unanswered why the Minister saw fit to subsequently implement one of them. This in itself raises serious questions surrounding the fitness for purpose of the new policy and whether it was implemented merely because it was the best of a bad lot.

Although driven by the Court's finding that here was an infringement of Article 8(2) of the Convention for the Protection of Human Rights and Fundamental Freedoms (hereafter the Convention), the Government has shied away from an outright declaration on homosexuality in the armed forces other than to lift the ban – something which required neither primary nor secondary legislation. Indeed the Code as it stands makes no mention of homosexuality using instead general terms designed to operate across a broad spectrum of scenarios. This leaves a number of very important questions unanswered. Mainly, given the nature of the Court and Convention does the Code satisfy the criticism levelled at the Government by the Court in *Lustig-Prean*? Will the implementation of the Code, given its broad scope and the subjective nature of the 'Service Test', satisfy the requirements of the Court and the Convention? Finally, and in light of recent case law,[7] how would the Court respond if it were faced with a case based upon disciplinary action brought under the Code in response to an allegation that someone's homosexuality had impacted on operational readiness?

THE CONVENTION AND THE HUMAN RIGHTS ACT

In order to understand more fully why a 'foreign' court has both the right and the ability to interfere with what are essentially operational matters we need to have at least a small appreciation of how the Convention and the Court work.

The Convention came into force in 1953 after the formation of the Council of Europe and in response to the need for greater elaboration of the obligations associated with Council membership. More generally, the birth of the Convention can be seen as a reaction to the events in Europe both before and after World War II and as an attempt to provide a bulwark against communism and its spread into Central and Eastern Europe. In addition to these factors the Convention was a direct reaction to the human rights atrocities witnessed during the war, with the perception that the Convention would act as a form of early warning system. In reality this last function of the Convention has remained largely inactive with only a small number of inter-state cases being brought.[8] The Convention has instead concentrated its efforts on isolated violations of human rights in those legal systems which are representative of the 'common heritage of political traditions, ideals, freedoms, and the rule of law' referred to in the Convention preamble.

Unlike the Universal Declaration of Human Rights, which divides human rights into civil and political rights on one hand, and socio-economic and cultural rights on the other, the Convention is predominantly concerned with the protection of civil and political rights.[9]

At an international level the Convention is a treaty, and as a treaty it must be interpreted in accordance with the international rules on the interpretation of treaties as found in the Vienna Convention.[10] The Vienna Convention lays down the basic requirement that a treaty:

> "shall be interpreted in good faith in accordance with the ordinary meaning to be given to the terms of the treaty in their context and in light of it's object and purpose".[11]

Accordingly considerable emphasis is placed upon interpreting the Convention using a teleological approach, that is an interpretation that seeks to realise its 'object and purpose'. In relationship to the Convention the Court has identified this as being 'the protection of individual human rights'[12] coupled to the maintenance and promotion of 'the ideals and values of a democratic society'.[13] Regarding the latter of these the Court has recognised that within a 'democracy' there exists the supposition that this includes 'pluralism, tolerance and broadmindedness'.[14] Finally, it must be noted that the Court does not overly concern itself with the rights of states other than to allow contracting states what is termed a 'margin of appreciation'. In general terms this gives a state a certain measure of discretion, subject to the Court and the Convention, when taking legislative, administrative or judicial action in those areas covered by the Convention.[15] Taken as a whole all these factors signify that:

> '[given] that this is a law-making treaty, it is also necessary to seek the interpretation that is most appropriate in order to realise the aim and achieve the object of the treaty, and not that which would restrict to the greatest degree the obligations undertaken by the parties'.[16]

Within the UK domestic legal order international treaties have no binding effect unless they are 'incorporated' into the legal order. This requires an Act of Parliament such as the European Communities Act 1972 which, generally speaking, gives effect to the laws of the European Union. The Convention, although ratified by the UK, has never been incorporated into UK law with the effect that a court has never been able to apply the provisions of the Convention directly.

With the introduction of the Human Rights Act in autumn of 2000 the position will change although not radically as the Human Rights Act does not in itself incorporate the Convention into UK law. The Human Rights Act will require courts to take various factors into account when determining a question that has arisen in connection with a Convention right, in particular the court will be under a duty to look at the following:

a. judgement[s], decision[s], declaration[s] or advisory opinion[s] of the European Court of Human Rights;
b. opinion[s] of the Commission in a report adopted under Article 31 of the Convention;
c. decision[s] of the Commission in connection with Article 26 or 27(2) of the Convention; or
d. decision[s] of the Committee of Ministers taken under Article 46 of the Convention.[17]

The Act then goes further in placing a duty on the court to interpret legislation in accordance with the Convention wherever possible. The stumbling block is the fact that the court is not empowered to set aside either primary or secondary legislation in favour of the Convention, neither are existing legislation or provisions deemed to be inferior to the Convention. The court is only empowered, by S.4, to make a declaration of incompatibility, something which is envisaged as having the effect of spurring Parliament into taking remedial action. The effect of such a declaration is questionable as S.4(6) bars the court from granting any effective judicial relief during this interim period between declaration and remedial legislation or action. Whilst by virtue of the same section the declaration does not affect the continuing validity of the provision in question.

> (6) A declaration under this section ("a declaration of incompatibility") –
> a. does not affect the validity, continuing operation or enforcement of the provision in respect of which it is given; and
> b. is not binding on the parties to the proceedings in which it is made.[18]

This leaves the individual in considerable doubt as to their legal position.

Although the armed forces have traditionally been insulated from the effects of both 'European' legislation and much of the philosophy which has driven the development of Europe in the 20th and 21st centuries, it is not a sustainable argument for anyone to claim that the Human Rights Act, and therefore the Convention, falls outside of the military sphere. On the contrary the Court has on many occasions felt the need to intervene in military matters and has stated that military service does not entail a cessation of rights,[19] it is certain that the Court would not entertain a defence based upon the non-applicability of either the Human Rights Act or the Convention.

As stated, the lifting of the ban on homosexuals serving in the armed forces required neither primary nor secondary legislation whilst its replacement is merely a code by which local commanders are to be guided. What degree of 'enforceability' local commanders see the Code as having remains to be seen; so too does the nature of any training that local commanders will receive in the interpretation and application of the Code. It is the quality of the training in dealing with the Code and the potential myriad of scenarios and pitfalls that will come out of it that will ultimately dictate the degree of success or failure of the Code. Alongside issues raised by the quality of any training that local commanders receive concerning the Code there is also the issue of awareness training for local commanders *vis-à-vis* the Human Rights Act. Whilst there appears to be no reason why local commanders should be aware of the Human Rights Act the reality is somewhat different. In particular the implementation of the Human Rights Act raises some serious issues in respect of the ability of local commanders to interpret military law in accordance with the Convention. Without discussing specific examples, local commanders must be made aware that whenever they are called upon to deal with an issue of homosexuality arising under the Code they are in fact dealing with what the Court has deemed to be the most intimate aspect of private life.[20] This will require local commanders to undertake their investigations and any subsequent disciplinary actions with the highest degree of 'fairness and impartiality'. The requirement of 'fairness and impartiality' in itself raises more doubts as to the ability of local commanders to comply with the provisions of both the Human Rights Act and the Convention. Again the Court has found the military judicial system lacking in these respects.[21]

Whilst it is unlikely that the Government would wilfully disregard a declaration of incompatibility, this does nothing to resolve the potential for harm given that Parliament often takes two or more years to bring legislation onto the statute books, or that Parliament may exercise its sovereign power and decide to preserve the status quo and decline to change an existing law, policy, or provision.

THE CODE: ITS EFFECTS AT NATIONAL LEVEL

In assessing the effects of the Code we are required to examine its wording and its potential operation in light of the ethos behind both the Court and Convention as well as in light of the potential effects of the forthcoming Human Rights Act.

The Code seeks to impose a strict moral regime on the armed forces, however, in attempting to do this it falls on the side of vagueness and subjectivity by giving broad band examples of conduct likely to fall within the remit of the Code. In doing this it also falls short of providing any form of legal certainty against which anyone can objectively judge the conduct of themselves or others. This uncertainty is further compounded by the fact that it will be for local commanders to judge the effects, or even the likely effects, of any conduct and whether such conduct falls within the Code. It is a relatively easy step to envisage a scenario where a local commander feeling that someone's conduct falls within the Code instigates disciplinary action. If that individual then having gone through the disciplinary process finds themselves dismissed from the armed forces it is highly possible that they will seek some form of judicial remedy. If the individual concerned is homosexual, regardless of whether or not the dismissal involves allegations of their homosexuality having an 'impact on the efficiency or operational effectiveness of the Service', they are unlikely to succeed in demonstrating that the only reason they were dismissed was because they were homosexual. On the other hand the Ministry of Defence would have a relatively easy task in showing that it was the impact of the individual's conduct (regardless of sexual orientation) which fell within the remit of the Code and was subsequently judged serious enough to warrant dismissal. Although appearing to lift the ban on homosexuals serving in the armed forces, at this juncture it is proposed that in reality the Government has put in place a moral regime under which homosexuality will still be regarded as having an unacceptable 'impact on the efficiency or operational effectiveness of the Service', whilst at the same time giving those who wish to discriminate against homosexuality the weapon with which to fight it. Even though the Code clearly makes no distinction between personnel of differing sexual orientation, merely imposing a blanket prohibition is unlikely to satisfy the requirements of the Court and the Convention regarding non-discrimination.

A further issue requiring examination is the statement by the Minister of Defence to Parliament on 12 January 2000. In his statement the Minister makes it clear that the ban on homosexuality could no longer be justified in light of recent judgements of the Court, but then moves on and states:

> "The code will apply across the forces, regardless of service, rank, gender or sexual orientation. It will provide a clear framework within which people in the services can live and work, and it will complement existing policies, such as zero tolerance towards harassment, discrimination and bullying. I emphasise that we are not tightening the rules on heterosexual relationships."[22]

The first and second parts of this paragraph are wholly consistent with those policies laid down in AFOPS.[23] They clearly demonstrate that 'regardless of service, rank, gender or sexual orientation' the Code will be applied evenly across all scenarios. However, the last part of this paragraph appears to contain an inconsistency that raises serious questions over the universal application of the Code. There is no question that the armed forces have always taken a serious view of morally reprehensible conduct, and providing such conduct was 'heterosexual' it was not regarded as unlawful per se. Therefore, in many ways the Minister is right in stating that Code does not tighten the rules on heterosexual relationships. However, the question remains as to why the Minister saw fit to include this last statement when previously he made it clear that the Code applied 'regardless of ... sexual orientation'. Either the Minister saw a need to reassure the heterosexual majority that in reality the Code makes little or even no difference to them; or else he was implying that in some way the Code has more applicability in cases involving homosexuality. In either case the message which the Minister is sending to local commanders and the judiciary alike is unclear.

With the Code itself being worded in such broad terms it is likely that any judge would seek some clarification regarding the 'object and purpose' of the Code. With the judiciary now having the opportunity to examine extracts from Hansard it is conceivable that a judge could interpret the Minister's statement as meaning heterosexual conduct was in some way more morally acceptable. The effects of this statement at a local level could be disastrous, certainly in light of the enormity of feeling against homosexuality in the armed forces[24] local commanders will be hard pushed to find that homosexuality does not in some way 'impact on the efficiency or operational effectiveness of the Service'.

A comparison can be drawn at this point between an 'idealistic' interpretation of the Code and the interpretation given by the courts to the Race Relations Act 1976. The Race Relations Act makes it unlawful to discriminate against anyone on racial grounds, furthermore it makes no allowance for discrimination which could in some way be held as being in the interests of the individual bringing the case. Therefore when Westminster City Council granted temporary employment to a black person but later withdrew it on the grounds that the workforce were threatening industrial action, the High Court had little trouble in backing the Commission for Racial Equality and finding that, regardless of motive, to give in to such threats would defeat the purpose of the Act.[25] Just as employing a black person brought about threats of industrial action in the *Westminster* case, homosexuality per se will always have some 'impact on the efficiency or operational effectiveness' within the service even if for no other reason than the attitudes held by some people towards living and working alongside someone of a different sexual orientation. Problems are most likely to arise when it is the issue of homosexuality itself, not someone's conduct, which leads, or is likely to lead, to an 'impact on...efficiency or operational effectiveness'. In these circumstances local commanders will be faced with essentially the same problem as Westminster City Council. Either they refuse to take action, in which case morale and operation effectiveness will suffer, or else they take some form of action and therefore discriminate against someone for no other reason than their sexual orientation.

Even the introduction of the Human Rights Act is unlikely to have a significant impact upon the position within the armed forces. There is no evidence to suggest that the armed forces disciplinary procedures will in the future give any credence to the requirements of the Human Rights Act, although to follow such a course of action would without doubt lead to a direct confrontation both with national courts and the Court itself. The unfortunate outcome is that personnel subjected to either lesser degrees of disciplinary action, or ultimately dismissed the service, are unlikely to find a satisfactory remedy within the armed forces judicial system. Only by taking the issue outside of the system will they stand any reasonable chance of obtaining a suitable remedy. This, however, does little to comfort those who had career aspirations within the armed forces and have found themselves dismissed. As long as the principal consideration in these matters remains efficiency and operational effectiveness (as quoted in the service test), and not a truly homogenous military structure vis-à-vis personal relationships, the armed forces will always maintain a collision course both with national courts and the Convention regarding the issue of homosexuality.

The introduction of the Code in its present form makes it difficult for the Government to justify its claims that homosexuality is no longer a bar to service in the armed forces. If we take a direct approach to non-discrimination in the armed forces it may be arguable that the lifting of the ban and the imposition of the Code ensures equal treatment vis-à-vis sexual orientation. However there are two issues which remain, firstly the indirect route left open by the Code by which some individuals and local commanders may make it impossible for homosexuals to serve openly in the armed forces; secondly the notion that whereas un-codified rules previously sufficed for heterosexual relationships only a code of conduct is sufficient to govern personal relationships when homosexuality is factored in. In either of the latter two cases the Code itself has the potential to be viewed as intrinsically discriminatory by both national courts and the Court of Human Rights.

CONFRONTATION: THE COURT, THE CONVENTION AND THE STATE

As previously discussed, the Court and the Convention give little leeway to states who plead issues of national security as a legitimate basis on which to infringe the rights of individuals.[26] In the *Lustig-Prean* case the applicants argued that the investigations into their homosexuality and their subsequent discharge from the Royal Navy, in pursuance of the absolute ban on homosexuals serving in the armed forces, amounted to an infringement of their rights under Article 8 of the Convention. Article 8 is formulated in two parts, it states:

1. "Everyone has the right to respect for his private and family life, his home and his correspondence.

2. There shall be no interference by a public authority with the exercise of this right except such as in accordance with the law and is necessary in a democratic society in the interests of national security, public safety or the economic well-being of the country, for the prevention of disorder or crime, for the protection of health or morals, or for the protection of the rights and freedoms of others."[27]

It can be seen from this that Article 8 is not an absolute prohibition against interference with private life, rather it allows states a 'margin of appreciation' when the interference justifiably falls within one of the exception contained in paragraph 2. It is important to note that the interference has to be justifiable and that it is for the Court not the state to determine what constitutes justifiable. The exceptions outlined in paragraph 2 are dealt with by the Court in the following manner; are they 'in accordance with the law' or 'prescribed by the law' and are they 'necessary in a democratic society' for the protection of one of the objectives set out in the second paragraph. These points themselves are dealt with by the Court in the order 'law', 'objective', and 'necessity'.

Each of these three requirements have been interpreted by the Court to the extent that 'in accordance with the law' requires the state to point to some specific legal rule or regime; 'for the protection of one of the objectives' requires the state to identify which 'objective' it is protecting by its interference; in dealing with 'necessity' the state must show that the interference is 'necessary in a democratic society', a phrase which weighs heavy with uncertainty. After a number of years in which this uncertainty prevailed the Court has finally decided on what the concept of 'necessary' constitutes:

"According to the Court's established case-law, the notion of necessity implies that an interference corresponds to a pressing social need and, in particular, that it is proportionate to the legitimate aim pursued."[28]

Coupled to the requirements set out above the Court also considers that the rights protected by the Convention form a hierarchy of rights, as such some rights and their infringement are considered of greater importance than others. Within the remit of Article 8 homosexuality is considered as being such an intimate aspect of private life as to warrant the greatest protection from state interference. The Court first referred to this in 1977 when it acknowledged the importance of untroubled sexual relations as a part of private life,[29] in 1981 the Court then went further in delineating exactly which 'sexual relations' fell within the remit of Article 8.

"The present case concerns [homosexuality] the most intimate aspect of private life. Accordingly, there must exist particularly serious reasons before interferences on the part of public authorities can be legitimate for the purposes of [Article 8(2)]."[30]

In deciding *Lustig-Prean* the Court considered the *Dudgeon* case cited above and held that neither the investigation into the applicants' homosexuality, nor the policy of the Ministry of Defence barring homosexuals serving in the armed forces, were justified under Article 8(2) of the Convention. The Court stated:

"Accordingly, when the relevant restrictions concern "a most intimate part of an individual's private life", there must exist "particularly serious reasons" before such interferences can satisfy the requirements of Article 8 § 2 of the Convention.

When the core of the national security aim pursued is the operational effectiveness of the armed forces, it is accepted that each state is competent to organise its own system of military discipline and enjoys a certain margin of appreciation in this. The Court also considers that it is open to the State to impose restrictions on an individual's right to respect for his private life where there is a real threat to the armed forces' operational effectiveness, as the proper functioning of an army is hardly imaginable without legal rules designed to prevent service personnel from undermining it. However, the national authorities cannot rely on such rules to frustrate the exercise by individual members of the armed forces of their right to respect for their private lives, *which right applies to service personnel as it does to others within the jurisdiction of the State.* Moreover, *assertions as to a risk to operational effectiveness must be "substantiated by specific examples."* [31] (Emphasis added)

The issue here is whether the Code, in relationship to the principles of 'necessity', 'margin of appreciation', and the judgement of the Court in *Lustig-Prean* is likely to elicit a more lenient approach from the Court. As discussed above the Code itself contains many flaws, not least of which is that it is intrinsically discriminatory, firstly by virtue of its highly subjective nature, and secondly because of the intimation by the Minister that there is in some way a delineation between heterosexual activity and homosexual activity. Certainly when these factors are taken into account it is unlikely that the Court would diverge from its previous case-law culminating in *Lustig-Prean*.

THE CODE, MILITARY TRIBUNALS AND THE CONVENTION

Throughout history and across all the countries of the world the armed forces have seen themselves as being in some way set apart from civilian judicial systems. Not only are the armed forces subject to civilian laws in addition they are subject to military laws and as such have developed a system of courts and tribunals by which to administer them. It has traditionally been the view of both military and civilian courts alike that the nature of the armed forces and service in them places service personnel in a less advantageous position vis-à-vis the civilian population. The ethos being that the nature of voluntary, or even conscript service in the armed forces in some way equates to a temporary cessation of certain rights on the part of service personnel. This view of service life as entailing certain restrictions and limitations, both imposed and accepted, has held sway for centuries and has without doubt led to service personnel falling into the second division with regard to rights. Only in the lifetime of the Convention has this view been challenged. The ethos of the Court and the Convention and the developing body of case-law have seen a shift away from this traditional view. The Court has led the way by developing a firm stance that service life does not entail any cessation of rights on the part of service personnel, and that states will be subjected to a narrow 'margin of appreciation' in cases involving service personnel. The impetus towards universal rights across both civilian and service personnel has received a considerable boost with the rapid development of the European Union. In particular the Court of Justice of the European Communities has openly stated that in matters concerning human rights it feels guided by the Court of Human Rights and its case-law.[32]

The two years prior to the latter part of 1999 saw a period of frenzied activity with the UK responding to claims laid before the court on a number of occasions.[33] In each of these cases the Court held that the military system of courts-martial did not constitute a fair or public hearing by an independent and impartial tribunal established by law, contrary to Article 6(1) of the Convention. Article 6(1) states:

> "In the determination ... of any criminal charge against him, everyone is entitled to a fair and public hearing ... by an independent and impartial tribunal established by law. ..."

Although the *Lustig-Prean* case did not revolve around Article 6(1) there is still a correlation that can be drawn between the Article 6 cases and *Lustig-Prean*. In particular with the Article 6 cases the Court held that a general court-martial, convened pursuant to the Army Act 1955, did not meet the requirements of independence and impartiality set down by Article 6(1) of the Convention in view of the central part played in its organisation by the convening officer. In this latter respect, the Court considered that the convening officer was central to the applicant's prosecution and was therefore too closely linked to the prosecution authorities. The Court expressed some concern that the members of the court-martial were subordinate (either directly or indirectly) to the convening officer, and the Court found it significant that the convening officer also acted as confirming officer. As such the Court was further of the opinion that, since the applicants' courts-martial had been found to lack independence and impartiality, they could not guarantee the applicants a fair trial. Although the Court has never been tasked with deciding on the fairness and impartiality of disciplinary actions other than courts-martial, these findings by the Court are to a large extent indicative of the military judicial system regardless of whether the issue at hand is a court-martial or some form of lesser disciplinary action.

The correlation then between these cases and *Lustig-Prean* is that the Court found that neither the investigations conducted into the applicants' sexual orientation, nor their discharge on the grounds of their homosexuality in pursuance of the Ministry of Defence policy, were justified. Had the Court been tasked with addressing the issues of fairness and impartiality (Article 6) it is highly probable that the Court would have found that the investigations and subsequent dismissals also fell short of the requirements laid down in Article 6. Given the previously discussed subjective nature of the 'Service Test', and the fact that it is for local commanders to assess the impact of 'personal relationships' on 'the efficiency or operational effectiveness of the Service', we are faced with essentially the same issue that the Court raised regarding the convening officer and his central part in the prosecution. This being that the local commander's part in any disciplinary action brought under the Code could well be seen as investing the trinity of judge, jury and executioner in one individual.

THE CODE AND THE RIGHT TO AN EFFECTIVE REMEDY

In relation to the Convention the lack of legal certainty (discussed above) generated by S.4 of the Human Rights Act is unlikely to be tolerated for long by the Court. Article 13 of the Convention requires the provision of an effective judicial remedy for anyone who considers that their Convention rights have been infringed.

"Everyone whose rights and freedoms as set forth in this Convention are violated shall have an effective remedy before a national authority not withstanding that the violation has been committed by persons acting in an official capacity."[34]

In applying Article 13 to scenarios involving the Code and homosexuality in the armed forces we are required to look at the principal requirements of Article 13. One of these is the requirement that the individual must consider that they have in some way been prejudiced by some act or measure which in itself constitutes a breach of the Convention:

" ... Article 13 requires that where an individual considers himself to have been prejudiced by a measure allegedly in breach of the Convention, he should have a remedy before a national authority in order to both have his claim decided and, if appropriate, to obtain redress."[35]

The second requirement is that the individual must have an 'effective remedy'. Effectiveness has four basic elements to it, any of which may have an impact on the other three, these are institutional, substantive, remedial and material effectiveness. Taking each of these points in turn the Court lays down criteria by which each will be judged. Institutional effectiveness requires that the decision-maker be sufficiently independent of the authority alleged to have violated the Convention. In this instance bodies such as the Courts-Martial Appeal Court would not be held as being sufficiently independent of the disciplinary process.[36] Within those constitutions that have given direct effect to the Convention the issue of substantive effectiveness is satisfied by the fact that an individual may raise the precise Convention provision directly before the national court. In those constitutions, such as the UK, where the Convention does not enjoy direct effect, the issue of substantive effectiveness requires that the individual is at least able to canvas the substance of the Convention provision before the national court. Therefore to deny an individual the right to argue discrimination on the grounds of homosexuality may constitute a breach of Article 13.

It is with the issue of remedial effectiveness that the Code and the Human Rights Act are most likely to fall foul of the

Convention. Remedial effectiveness requires that a national authority be in a position to grant the individual a remedy if it accepts the individual's argument. The requirement of remedial effectiveness will not be satisfied if any potential remedy relies on a wholly discretionary response either from the national authority itself, or from another national decision-making body.[37] A declaration of incompatibility under S.4 of the Human Rights Act has no legal status by which to force Parliament into action, Parliament's decision either to action or not is therefore wholly discretionary and as such fails to satisfy the requirements laid down in Article 13 and the case-law of the Court.

The final requirement, that of material effectiveness, requires that where a right of appeal lies to a sufficiently independent body then the individual must make use of that right of appeal before petitioning the Court. The view that the Court has taken of the military appeals system would suggest that the requirement of material effectiveness is unlikely to be satisfied. The result is that an individual would not have to seek the right of appeal if that right lay only with the Courts-Martial Appeal Court.

Although the current state of affairs vis-à-vis the UK and the Convention is highly problematical it must be said that the eventual development of a body of case-law under the forthcoming Human Rights Act will go a long way in alleviating many of the problems currently faced by both civilian and service applicants alike. For the UK the non-implementation of the Convention into national law, its limited direct effect under the Human Rights Act, and the discretionary nature of much public power coupled to the largely unintrusive nature of judicial control, means that the provisions of Article 13 have an important part to play in protecting individual rights under the Convention. It is envisaged that the Human Rights Act will act as a strong incentive for the courts, both civilian and military, in encouraging an approach that is sensitive to the Convention and the rights it protects.

CONCLUSION

Few would doubt that the highly discriminatory state of affairs that held sway under the pre-existing order could continue for much longer. The UK had for some time been amongst the minority of European states in still operating a blanket ban on homosexuals serving in the armed forces. Indeed by the time the Court gave the *Lustig-Prean* judgement apart from the UK only Turkey and Luxembourg, and possibly Greece and Portugal, operated any form of ban. The growing number of cases of discrimination on the grounds of homosexuality and the Government's own admissions relating to the potential numbers of homosexuals serving in the armed forces[38] demonstrated that sooner rather than later the policy of operating a blanket ban would have to change. All that remained once the Court gave its judgement in *Lustig-Prean* was to see when the change in policy would take place and in what form.

The indications from the report of the Homosexuality Policy Assessment Team are that the Government had a number of possible solutions by which they could have resolved the issue of homosexuality in the armed forces. Given that this report was published in February 1996 there is strong evidence that coupled to the mounting numbers of individuals dismissed for homosexuality, the Government were fully aware that the policy of exclusion had a limited life left to run, and had been so aware for some time. When in 1996 the HPAT concluded that in reality there was little, or at least no realistic alternative to the ban the Government should have considered themselves as being on notice that the ban was running into trouble and should therefore have allocated sufficient resources to solving the problem. The indications are that the Government and the armed forces took the path of least resistance, the Government by promising to put the matter before Parliament for a free vote but only after the next Parliamentary Select Committee review of the policy in 2001, and the armed forces via the HPAT and its rather unhelpful decision that there was no alternative to a highly discriminatory ban.

One issue that remains far from clear is the position of the Government vis-à-vis its perception of the *Lustig-Prean* case and its chances of obtaining a satisfactory outcome. The statement made by the Defence Secretary on 12 January 2000 contains a passage which in itself is difficult to reconcile with the reality of the situation. The Minister states that as a result of the *Lustig-Prean* judgement he had requested the Chief of the Defence Staff to conduct an urgent review of policy. The outcome of this urgent review, as already seen, is the implementation of the Code, something which the HPAT dismissed in 1996 as being unworkable. The feeling here is that the Government may have been caught out by the Court's decision in *Lustig-Prean* in as much as they may have felt that the case would be decided in their favour. Left with a policy in shreds and a potential political embarrassment if they were seen to do nothing, the Government did indeed ask the Chief of the Defence Staff to conduct an 'urgent' review, however, this review consisted of nothing more than dredging up previously discarded ideas and re-presenting them as a panacea for what in reality was a lack of enthusiasm on the parts of the Government and the military to tackle this particular political minefield.

All these issues have and will continue to contribute to the problems faced by the Code, its application, and its reputation. The next test for the Code will come when the Human Rights Act becomes law in the autumn of 2000. There appears to have been little or no consideration on the part of the policy review team regarding the impact of such a piece of legislation when it suggested in January 2000 that the Minister implement the Code. Whilst the Human Rights Act remains a Bill it can have no impact within the UK legal order. However, all this is set to change when the Bill finally makes it to the Statute books. At that time all those fulfilling judicial or pseudo-judicial roles will find their decision-making processes influenced whenever the issue before them has a 'Convention' dimension. Regardless of whether the status of the judicial function is civilian or military the influence of the Human Rights Act will be felt at every level. Given that the armed forces have generated a significant workload for the Court, it would be inconceivable for anyone to suggest that the Human Rights Act did not, or could not, be applied evenly across both the military and civilian judicial functions. Any attempt by either the Government or the armed forces to exclude the application of the Human Rights Act would set both on a course of confrontation with the Court. Again the Government would face the potential embarrassment of the Court finding that the Government's policy was contrary to 'the protection of individual human rights' and 'the ideals and values of a democratic society'.

This is not to say that the Human Rights Act is in anyway a cure-all for the lack of well-defined human rights within the UK legal order. Whereas most countries have opted to incorporate the Convention into their legal orders, and by doing so given the Convention direct-effect, the Government has in reality done little in the way of giving the Convention any effect, direct or otherwise. The notion that somehow an individual's rights are better protected by a court whose only remedy is to inform Parliament of an incompatibility between UK provisions and the Convention provisions, is nonsensical. Had the Human Rights Act been in force when Mr Lustig-Prean initially found himself in conflict with the authorities the eventual outcome would have been no different. The armed forces would still have continued with the administrative action to dismiss him, whilst the outcome of any legal action before a civilian court would at best have resulted in a declaration of incompatibility under S.4 of the Human Rights Act. Had Parliament chosen not to act on this declaration then the case of *Lustig-Prean and Beckett v. the United Kingdom* would undoubtedly have been decided in the same way. The only difference this time would be that the Court would most likely find both a breach of Article 8(2) – the right to private life, and a further breach of Article 13 – the right to an effective remedy.

As discussed, the lack of thought and foresight that appears to have gone into the formulation and introduction of the Code leaves it in a position of substantial vulnerability vis-à-vis the Human Rights Act and the Convention. The wording of the Code and in particular the 'Service Test', which asks local commanders to make a value judgement as to the impact or likely impact of an individual's conduct, remains highly subjective. The provisions of the Convention will remain unsatisfied whenever there is the slightest indication that a local commander's decision may in some way be based upon discrimination or that they have failed to demonstrate that sexual orientation had no part in their decision. It is proposed that the degree of 'fairness' and 'impartiality' that local commanders will have to exercise in their decision-making processes if they are not to fall foul of the Human Rights Act, the Convention, and the Court are outside of their capabilities as managers. This in no way decries their capabilities as military commanders; rather it highlights the almost impossible task that the Government has placed in their hands.

In summary then, it is proposed that the armed forces have moved from a position of utmost certainty under a total ban on homosexuality to a position where there exists considerable uncertainty as to the acceptability of the issue of sexual orientation and its impact on the operation of the armed forces. This lack of clarity and the Code's highly subjective nature leaves the door of opportunity open to those that wish to continue the policy of discrimination based on sexual orientation. Although it is unlikely that this was the intent behind the Code this is the reality.

NOTES

1. *Lustig-Prean and Beckett v. the United Kingdom.* Application nos. 31417/96 and 32377/96. 27th September 1999.
2. Hansard. 12th January 2000. Column 285 – 287.
3. Code of Conduct. http://www.mod.uk/policy/homosexuality/index.html.
4. Ibid.
5. Ibid.
6. *Lustig-Prean.* Op. cit. para. 54.
7. *Cable and Others v. the United Kingdom.* Application nos.

00024436/94;	00024582/94;	00024583/94;	00024584/94;	00024895/94;
00025937/94;	00025939/94;	00025940/94;	00025941/94;	00026271/95;
00026525/95;	00027341/95;	00027342/95;	00027346/95;	00027357/95;
00027389/95;	00027409/95;	00027760/95;	00027762/95;	00027772/95;
00028009/95;	00028790/95;	00030236/96;	00030239/96;	00030276/96;
00030277/96;	00030460/96;	00030461/96;	00030462/96;	00031399/96;
00031400/96;	00031434/96;	00031899/96;	00032024/96;	00032944/96.

18th February 1999.
Coyne v. the United Kingdom. Application no. 00025942/94. 24th September 1999.
Moore and Gordon v. the United Kingdom. Application nos. 00036529/97 and 00037393/97. 29th September 1999.
Smith and Ford v. the United Kingdom. Application nos. 00037475/97 and 00039036/97. 29th September 1999.
8. So far 11 inter-state cases have been brought before the Commission.
9. Articles 1 and 2, First Protocol address guarantees of the rights to property and education.
10. Vienna Convention on the Law of Treaties 1969.
11. Article 31, Vienna Convention.
12. *Soering v UK.* A 161 para. 87 (1989).
13. *Kjeldsen, Busk Madsen and Pedersen v Denmark.* A 23 para. 53 (1976).
14. *Handyside v UK.* A 24 para. 49 (1976).
15. Ibid.

16. *Wemhoff v FRG.* A 7 p. 23 (1968).
17. S.2(1) Human Rights Act 1998.
18. Ibid.
19. See below for a detailed discussion of this point.
20. Ibid.
21. Ibid.
22. Hansard. 12th January 2000. Column 285 – 287.
23. Armed Forces Overarching Personnel Strategy.
24. The Report of the Homosexuality Assessment Team. Feb. 1996. Quoted in *Lustig-Prean and Beckett v. the United Kingdom.* Application nos. 31417/96 and 32377/96. 27th September 1999 at paras 45 and 51.
25. *R v. CRE ex parte Westminster City Council* [1985] IRLR 426, CA.
26. For an example of this see: *McCann and others v. United Kingdom.* Application 18984/91. 3rd September 1993. IRA suspects killed on Gibraltar.
27. Article 8 European Convention for the Protection of Human Rights and Fundamental Freedoms.
28. *Olsson v. Sweden.* A 24 para. 48.
29. *Bruggeman and Scheuten v. FRG.* Application no. 6959/77.
30. *Dudgeon v. UK.* A 45 para. 52.
31. *Lustig-Prean* at para. 82.
32. EU Law. Text Cases and Materials. Craig and De Burca. 2nd Edition. Oxford. 1998 at page 296.
33. See cases; Findlay v. the United Kingdom judgment of 25 February 1997, *Reports of Judgments and Decisions* 1997-I, pp. 272–5, §§ 32–51;
    Cable and others v. UK Application nos.
    00024436/94;   00024582/94;   00024583/94;   00024584/94;   00024895/94;
    00025937/94;   00025939/94;   00025940/94;   00025941/94;   00026271/95;
    00026525/95;   00027341/95;   00027342/95;   00027346/95;   00027357/95;
    00027389/95;   00027409/95;   00027760/95;   00027762/95;   00027772/95;
    00028009/95;   00028790/95;   00030236/96;   00030239/96;   00030276/96;
    00030277/96;   00030460/96;   00030461/96;   00030462/96;   00031399/96;
    00031400/96; 00031434/96; 00031899/96; 00032024/96; 00032944/96;
    Coyne v. UK 00025942/94
    Moore and Gordon v. UK Application nos. 00036529/97; 00037393/97
    Smith and Ford v. UK Application nos. 00037475/97; 00039036/97
34. Article 13 European Convention for the Protection of Human Rights and Fundamental Freedoms.
35. *Klass v. FRG.* A 28 para. 64 (1979).
36. *Moore and Gordon v. UK* Application nos. 00036529/97; 00037393/97
37. *Silver v. UK.* A 61 paras. 54, 115. (1983) and *Campbell and Fell v. UK.* A 80 paras 51, 126 (1984).
38. *Lustig-Prean* at para. 60.

Index

For Product Safety Concerns and Information please contact our EU
representative GPSR@taylorandfrancis.com
Taylor & Francis Verlag GmbH, Kaufingerstraße 24, 80331 München, Germany

www.ingramcontent.com/pod-product-compliance
Ingram Content Group UK Ltd.
Pitfield, Milton Keynes, MK11 3LW, UK
UKHW040836280425
457818UK00030B/315